Marriage Made in Heaven

Marriage Made in Heaven

The Story of Billy and Ruth Graham

by

Jhan Robbins

HODDER AND STOUGHTON
LONDON   SYDNEY   AUCKLAND   TORONTO

The author gratefully acknowledges permission from the following sources to quote material in the text:

Sojourners for material from 'A Change of Heart', an interview conducted by Jim Wallis and Wes Michaelson (August 1979), in *Sojourners* magazine, P.O. Box 29262, Washington, D.C., 20017.
Word Books, Waco, Texas, for two poems from *Sitting by My Laughing Fire*, by Ruth Bell Graham, copyright © 1977 by Ruth Bell Graham.

British Library Cataloguing in Publication Data

Robbins, Jhan
  Marriage made in heaven.—(Hodder Christian paperback)
  1. Graham, Billy   2. Graham, Ruth
  3. Evangelists—United States—Biography
  4. Clergymen's wives—United States—Biography
  I. Title
  269'.2'0922   BV3785.G69

ISBN 0 340 35174 8

To Steve Stout
Pastor
Goldsboro Friends Meeting
Goldsboro, N.C.

"Thee are loving to all."

CONTENTS

FOREWORD

Regardless of the views you now hold on Billy Graham, your marriage can be strengthened through closer acquaintance with the controversial evangelist and by getting to know his remarkable wife, Ruth Bell Graham, and their extraordinary marital relationship. It is likely you will go away from this book able to build a better marriage of your own.

Billy and Ruth Graham share a tender, productive, intimate alliance. It is of deep fire and great strength, built on patience, respect and prayer. President Lyndon Johnson called them, "Envied possessors of a near-flawless marriage." He said, "Balance is one word that describes that marriage. As helpmeets they are even-steven. They never seem to get out of kilter even when one surprises and dismays the other. Once, when they were our houseguests at the White House, I asked during dinner if Billy would give me the name of a good vice-presidential candidate. Instead of answering my question he shot out of his chair and yelled, 'Ruth, why did you just kick me under the table?'

"She winced in embarrassment. Then she took a deep breath and said quietly, 'Bill, shouldn't you limit your advice to spiritual matters?'

"The average husband," Johnson continued, "would have been annoyed by his wife's interference. Billy reached across the table and squeezed her hand. Then he looked at her lovingly. Later, Lady Bird said, 'I would have liked to have had a snapshot showing Ruth's reaction and Billy's—two beautiful smiles derived from *really* living together.' "

Dr. Karl Barth, the noted Swiss theologian, shared President Johnson's opinion about the Graham union. Dr. Barth said, "I've observed first-hand their bonds of marriage—a true mixture of God, love and respect."

Almost any wife would be ecstatic to discover that influential people were offering her husband huge financial support to run for the presidency of the United States. She would display a sudden passion for Rolls-Royces on learning that a prominent Hollywood director wanted to star him in an epic extravaganza. She might well plunk down a deposit on a lavish country estate when told that the chairman of a major television network was urging him to sign a million-dollar-per-year contract to host a talk show.

Ruth Graham's husband, Billy, turned down all three proposals. "Your bounded duty to the Lord is elsewhere," she reminded him.

Over the years I have written numerous newspaper stories and magazine articles about Billy Graham. I have talked to critics, associates and friends of the evangelist and his wife. Some of the things they divulged sounded too good to be true. When I told Graham that as an investigating Quaker journalist I was going to search for blemishes, he smiled. "I'm certain they exist," he said. "I won't get to heaven without bearing any scars. No human can!"

The list of the people who were helpful is so numerous that it is difficult to acknowledge them all. I'll simply say, "Many thanks to everybody." However, a special note of appreciation goes to my wife, Sallie Prugh, for her dedicated encouragement; to Robert Shuster and Frances Brocker, of the Billy Graham Center at Wheaton College, for their valuable aid that was often beyond normal assistance; to the Reverend Dr. Glenn Henricksen for reading the manuscript and offering useful suggestions; to June Reno, for judicious editing; and to Anne Angelo for typing the final version.

JHAN ROBBINS

Shortly after I completed this book, Harry Prugh, my father-in-law, died. He was the finest Christian I ever knew. Before I undertook this project I told him that I had some reservations about Billy Graham—there were areas of disagreement. Harry said, "If Billy Graham has the ability to help people live more satisfactory lives, perhaps you should do it." I'm glad I took his advice.

J. R.

Marriage Made in Heaven

1
THE WAYWARD BOY
AND THE CHINA GIRL

Billy

"BILLY FRANK'S EARLY hero was not Jesus Christ," said
Morrow Graham, the evangelist's mother. "It was Babe Ruth!
How much he wanted to become a famous baseball player!
His long legs made the idea dimly promising. He was always
practicing with the ball. He lived on the sandlot. In his
dreams, he'd mutter, 'Strike two!' In those days that was all
he was keen on—unless you include girls. He often said to
me, 'There are three things I don't want to be when I get
older: a milkman, an undertaker, or a preacher!' "

Graham did, briefly, play a few $10-a-game semiprofes-
sional baseball games for a local team. It's been said that he
was scouted by several major-league teams. That, to his
everlasting regret, is not so. He was never a strong enough
batter to be taken seriously. However, one of his evangelistic
crusades took him to Yankee Stadium, the baseball park that
is often called "the House that Babe Ruth built." When Billy
was introduced, the audience of 100,000 greeted him with

thunderous applause. Despite the temperature hovering at 105 degrees, the excited crowd cheered for more than ten minutes.

Yankee manager Casey Stengel attended the service. Stengel, whose mixed metaphors are as famous as his management, told reporters, "I saw more yelling and hand clapping than the Babe ever got for belting a homer. That Billy-boy sure is twenty-four-carat classy in a league that really counts like milk is healthy for a baby."

Graham's association with clamor started at birth. A neighbor who observed the new baby said, "I've brought dozens of babies into this world, but I've never heard a newborn squall so loud. You could practically hear this one all the way to the center of town!"

The noisy infant was born at home on November 7, 1918, four days before the end of World War I. At the time, his father, William Franklin Graham, Sr., exulted to a friend, "This baby is sure to bring luck. Soon we'll see a finish to all the fighting in Europe."

Home was a 300-acre dairy farm in Charlotte, North Carolina, which the elder Graham had inherited from his parents. The large tract of rolling hills and pastureland is now a shopping center, bordered by multistoried office buildings. The only reminder of its rural past is a memorial plaque:

Birthplace of Dr. Billy Graham
Born November 7, 1918
World Renowned Evangelist, Author and Educator
Preacher of the Gospel of Christ
to more people than any other man in history

Following a brief honeymoon, William Senior brought his bride, Morrow Coffey, to the farm, which then was five miles beyond the town line. She was also "country bred," and had always lived in that agricultural district. Like her husband she was descended from Scottish farmers who had settled in the Carolinas 250 years ago when the lands were still colonies of the English Crown. One of her ancestors was a signer of the Declaration of Independence. Another, James Knox Polk, was the eleventh President of the United States.

Ben Coffey, Morrow's father, was a Confederate Army veteran, who lost an eye and a leg at Gettysburg. He was a cavalryman in General Pickett's famed, gallant charge. The badly wounded Coffey, nonanesthetized, was about to be removed from the operating table when he noticed his severed right leg resting in a corner—still wearing a boot.

"He accepted the loss as God's will," said Morrow. "He was a very reverent person. My mother was that way, too. We regularly read the Bible in our house and had daily prayers together as a family. We were looking for the Lord's return. It was instilled in us—faith that Jesus was coming back. We went to church each Sabbath."

Billy's paternal grandfather was different. Crook Graham, also a Civil War veteran, believed that Sunday had been invented solely for whiskey. "He drank and swore and had little time for the Lord," said the evangelist. "Fortunately, his wife was a God-fearing woman. She read her Bible every day and taught the Word of God to her eight daughters and three sons. Through her influence, all her children became Christians."

"It has been carried on," said Morrow. "Billy Frank and his

17

brother and sisters were reared in a house where we put our faith in the Bible. We felt that what the Bible said was the only right way to live. I can still hear my husband telling Billy Frank, 'Every word of God is pure: *A wise son heareth his father's instruction.*' "

A hired man who helped tend the Graham's handsome herd of Jersey and Holstein cows said, "For a long while religion and Billy Frank didn't mix. The boy did pretty much what other kids do—only maybe more because he was bigger. He'd always run instead of walk—like he had to get somewhere in a special hurry. He'd rush into you like the way a bull charges a pair of red bloomers. One time he piled his father into some fresh cement. Was Mr. Graham mad! Took off his belt. When it was all over Billy Frank was sweet as pie. But the very next day he was up to his old tricks. Only this time I was the aggravated party—he made me fall into a pile of manure."

When the youngster wasn't knocking over everything in his way, he engaged in other forms of mischief. The family attended a very straitlaced Presbyterian church. "When I was a kid," the evangelist said, "I used to think that preachers all wore dark suits and long faces."

One Sunday, in the midst of the sermon, Billy made use of a large rubber band and a pocketful of paper pellets. His special targets were the heads of bald worshipers. On Sunday afternoons following church, Billy was forbidden to read newspaper comics or play games.

Often, he defied these orders. Neighbors remember that when he was certain his parents weren't looking, he'd pretend he was Tarzan of the Apes. He'd jump off the back porch and race for the trees. Then he'd climb one, let out a piercing yell and swing from branch to branch. Discovered, he would obediently vault down, pause a moment, then become one of Theodore Roosevelt's Rough Riders, storming up San Juan Hill. His imagination was wild, with himself always the dramatic hero.

At age six he had so much excess energy that his worried mother hauled him to a local doctor. "My boy never runs down," she complained. After a careful examination the report was: "Premature growing pains."

Morrow felt that schooling might help calm the youngster down. She had spent a year in college and greatly respected academics. Billy was enrolled in the Sharon Grammar School. Promptly at 7 A.M., on the first morning of the new term, she took him to the bus stop. He was uncomfortably dressed in a starched white shirt, blue tie and gray checked knickers. Morrow handed him a lunchbox that she had packed. "Eat it during the noon recess," she called as the yellow bus pulled out.

When Billy entered his classroom he took a back-row seat. The bell rang, indicating the start of the school day. He thought it signaled the lunch recess. As the teacher called the roll, he quietly ate the peanut butter sandwich and apple his mother had given him. During the proper noon recess, four hours later, a very hungry Billy looked enviously at his classmates as they devoured their food.

Going to school presented new problems. He was the tallest boy in class but he was also the thinnest. One of the other students called him "A skinny marink!" and challenged him to a fistfight. Billy was the clear loser, with a black eye and scraped chin. "I got the worst beating of my life," he recalls. After several more such defeats, Billy found his expertise—he could outrun anybody in the school.

He also discovered that he liked girls. His first sweetheart was the freckled, pigtailed lass who sat next to him in class: "She was brilliant as well as athletic," he recalled. "She was a real tomboy. Puppy love is laughed at by adults, but it is very real to a puppy."

Because of his height, Graham was given the role of Uncle Sam in a seventh grade school play. Barbara Linker, one of his classmates, remembers that first public appearance: "Most of us whooped it up when Billy came on stage. The white whiskers he was wearing kept falling down. He looked more like a worried, overgrown Jackie Cooper than Uncle Sam."

The evangelist's recollection of that performance was a pair of knocking knees and perspiring hands. "I vowed," he said, "that I would never again appear in public."

One Christmas he was given a bicycle. After hours of tumbling, he learned to stay right side up, and high speed became paramount. "He caused several of the farm animals to feel that way too," his brother Melvin recalled. "I'd watch him peddling furiously down the road, followed by an out-of-breath goat, a panting collie and a flock of exhausted chickens." (Billy has three very attractive younger siblings—Melvin, Catherine and Jean.)

The evangelist has made good use of memories of his bicycle technique, and often includes them in his sermons: "I found there was one thing to do on that bike if I wanted to stay on it. I had to keep moving forward. If I stopped moving forward, I would fall off and hurt myself. A Christian must learn that. He must keep moving forward in his faith."

Returning from one of the bicycle cavalcades, he was observed and admired by a hired hand. "Anybody who can do that," the man said, "deserves a reward." He reached in his breast pocket and took out a plug of chewing tobacco and handed it to the delighted and flattered youngster. William, Sr., discovered Billy chewing away. He promptly ordered him to spit, unbuckled his belt and fired the offending employee.

"I guess," said Billy, "that until I was about fourteen I was on the receiving end of quite a few thrashings. My father used his belt. Mother preferred a long hickory switch. If I broke a rule, they never hesitated. But as I look back I realize that the rules were fair. Sometimes I'm sure the things I did— or didn't do—must have been exasperating to them, but they never spanked me without good reason. And believe me, I gave them plenty of reasons."

A teacher once told Morrow Graham, "Your son isn't a very good student. I'll ask him to recite something and he won't even answer. I've had to chase him around my desk and whack him with a ruler to settle him down. The boy lacks drive. He needs to learn to apply himself."

When Billy's mother urged him to study harder, he would shuffle his feet and protest, "Why do I need to be educated? My father is a farmer, and so was his father. That's what I'll be. A farmer don't need any book learning!" As if to prove his point, he was already handy around the barn. Each morning he rose at 3 A.M. to help tend the cows and deliver the milk. Then he ate breakfast and headed for school.

Secretly, he hoped to become a big-league baseball player.

He has said that the reason so many star athletes have come from North Carolina was because "making it in baseball" was one of the few ways they could hope to beat the state's hard times.

He was very excited when he learned that Babe Ruth was coming to Charlotte to exhibit his slugging skill with a baseball bat. He pleaded with his father to take him to see the famous hitter. The Reverend Dr. Grady Wilson, a boyhood friend and currently a close associate, recalls, "Mr. Graham bought tickets for Billy and a number of his pals. He arranged for Billy to shake hands with the great King of Swat. Billy didn't wash his hand for three days."

The opposite sex was as impressed with the tall, handsome youngster as he was with baseball. The romance with his pigtailed classmate was succeeded by naive love affairs with many other girlfriends. "The list was long," his mother said. "He'd sit down at the supper table and sigh. That was a sure sign of what would follow: he'd smile shyly and tell us, 'I've just met the cutest girl ever!' "

One of them was Pauline Presson, the pretty daughter of the town's leading contractor. "She was my first *real* romance," Billy said. "I was fifteen when I met her. She was more sophisticated than any other girl I had ever dated. She was lovely and knew how to make herself even lovelier. But never in a flashy way. It was fun to be with her—we laughed a great deal."

Pauline remembers him as a tall, blond, extremely good-looking boy with a wonderful grin: "He was so handsome. He could have been in the movies, I thought. Nice to be with. Didn't cuss or act rough the way some of the other boys behaved. He'd never call for me in blue jeans. In the summertime he wore dark blue trousers, a white jacket and white shoes. Never without a tie. Although I must say that some of those ties were pretty wild. He always liked fancy clothes."

The young couple went to church socials in his father's Plymouth. "Afterwards," said Billy, "we'd drive to some secluded spot and park. We held hands and kissed while listening to the radio music of Tommy Dorsey and Glenn Miller."

In those days North Carolina had no age requirements for driving. Billy's idea of fun was to borrow the family automobile and joyride on the sidewalk. He drove around curves on two wheels. He drove across pastures. Once he got his father's car mired in deep mud, and the elder Graham had to use mules to pull it out. Billy's friends drove with the same abandon. He remembers standing up in the rear seat of a fast-moving convertible, one hand around his date and the other madly ringing a cowbell.

"I'm not trying to justify my actions," said Billy, "but remember this was during the great depression of the thirties. Hundreds of thousands of people walked the streets looking for work. Heads of families sold apples on street corners. Hitler was on the march across Europe. Ethiopia had fallen to Mussolini. Manchuria had been invaded. A few 'ridiculous' men were predicting a second world war. I understood little, and like young people today resented my parents, my teachers, my humdrum life as a farmhand and high school student."

"He was always getting into hot water," recalled a high

23

school bus driver. "A couple of times a week, when Billy and his friends got off the bus, he'd reach underneath and turn off the shutoff valve of the gas tank. I'd drive about a hundred yards and the engine would sputter out. I'd get out and shake my fist at him, but he'd only give me the laughing yanh-yanhs. He was a hero to his schoolmates!"

"By today's standards," the evangelist says, "this sort of misbehavior would be dismissed as 'youthful friskiness.' But try to remember, at that time, my community considered them extremely wild. I'm afraid everyone agreed we teenagers were doomed, especially 'that Billy Graham.' My parents were plenty worried. I gave them a hard time."

In the spring of 1934, concerned local farmers, Graham Senior included, and local businessmen, decided that a powerful stimulant was needed to combat wantonness and spiritual apathy. They erected a temporary tabernacle and invited fundamentalist preacher Mordeci Ham to conduct prayer meetings. The Reverend Ham specialized in the spiritual rescue of the decadent populations of southern cities. He assured the anxious town fathers that the entire community could soon look forward to purification and salvation. For eleven weeks the tempestuous revivalist thundered about eternity and redemption. He fastened in his talk on the devil's big three temptations: dancing, card playing and whiskey.

Ham indicted all of the Charlotte high school students. He claimed they would surely be damned to hell if they didn't instantly mend their deceitful ways. "Fornication on campus is rampant!" he raged. "You are all sinners!"

The accusations brought out an angry mob of teenagers—

Graham included—intent on forcing the evangelist to retract his charges. Instead, the provoked students meekly took seats in the makeshift tabernacle and listened respectfully.

Billy was spellbound. The following evening he returned; soon he became a steady visitor. Although he was not guilty of any of the vices Ham spoke of, he felt he had to promise to give them up. One night while the choir was singing "Almost Persuaded," the sixteen-year-old Billy stepped forward asking to be saved: "The grip of an old-fashioned revival is hard to explain. People are seized by a unity of consecration far more intense than occurs during any regular service. Each listener becomes deeply involved with the evangelist, who describes your sins—somehow he knows—and shortcomings and demands on pain of Divine Judgment that you mend your ways. As I listened, I began to have thoughts I had never known before. Something began to speak to my heart."

One of the first things Billy did when he returned home was to throw his arms around his mother. "I am a changed boy!" he told her. The next day, when he attended class, one of his teachers said, "Preacher Graham, will you explain the lesson? I hear you got religion last night!"

He was quieter in school and his grades improved somewhat, although he still ranked near the bottom of his class. He managed to graduate "by the skin of my teeth," he recalled. "I suspect I squeezed through because my father was a member of the school board."

Billy worried: he still liked girls. He had no intention of becoming a minister, despite his mother's urging, yet he found himself berating friends who he felt were leaning toward the devil. When one of them said, "Goddamn," he became enraged. "Don't ever blaspheme in my presence!" he shouted. "You know that I am a Christian!" At a high school class party he observed his current girlfriend dancing, waltzing with the host's father. "Stop immediately!" Billy ordered. "Dancing leads toward sin!"

The friends he saw often were, like himself, newly converted. The group became known as the "Preacher Boys." Several of them planned to attend Bob Jones College, an uncredited, ultra-fundamentalist Bible school, then located in Cleveland, Tennessee. Billy decided that he would also go there. To help pay expenses he got a temporary job as a Fuller Brush salesman. His assignment took him to South Carolina where he prayed before ringing doorbells. "The results," said John Davidson, a fellow salesman, "were amazing. He'd put his big foot in the door and not take no for an answer. His spiel worked so well that the company wanted to keep him on permanently."

"You may not think so," Graham said, "but I'm naturally sort of a shy fellow. Introverted. Selling brushes got me over some of that. It allowed me to talk with people and to sell people. My technique was to offer a free brush—in those days that was a big thing. I would have to empty my whole case of brushes to get to the free one. The woman would invariably inquire, 'By the way, what's this?' or 'How much is that?' Well, I knew I had a fish on a string. I don't want to sound too commercial. The truth is that I felt I was doing her a favor. I had become convinced that Fuller brushes were the best in the world and no family should be without them."

Billy often earned more than $50 a week—an excellent income in the mid-thirties. When he felt that he had accumulated enough money, he enrolled as a freshman in Bob Jones College. Dressed in red and white sport jacket, wide, light-gray trousers, a pepper-and-salt bow tie and maroon suede shoes, he arrived on campus.

He was disappointed at what he found there. The school was an ultimate in strictness and rigidity. Male and female students were so segregated that it was against the rules even to speak to the opposite sex. They had to keep their bodies at least six inches apart, demerits were given for loitering in the hall, and a sign was posted in each dormitory room: GRIPING NOT TOLERATED!

Once Billy told the head of the college, Dr. Bob Jones, that he was unhappy. Jones' reply was, "If you're a misfit here, you'll be a misfit anywhere . . . chances are you'll never amount to much."

When the semester ended, a demoralized Billy Graham returned home. His appearance was frail. His mother was dismayed: "He was always thin, but this was frightening. In addition, he had a bad cough." She took her son to a doctor, who advised lots of sunshine.

Billy's former roommate, Wendell Phillips, had transferred to the Florida Bible Institute near Tampa, Florida. It was decided that Billy Frank should also go there. The new school was a complete change. Also uncredited, it was less rigid. "Ninety students and our teachers lived together," the evangelist recalled. "A big happy family. We all worked together. We washed dishes, raked leaves, shined shoes. Everybody liked and respected everybody else."

One student Billy especially liked was a pretty, slender, brunette sophomore. He was in love again. This time the object of his affection was Emily Regina Cavanaugh, described by classmates as "beautiful, talented and spiritual." She and her two sisters had formed a gospel singing trio and performed at churches and local radio stations.

Together, Emily and Billy attended religious meetings and lectures. Each evening, before dinner, they would meet in the student lounge to discuss religion and prayer. "I was very, very impressed with the way he prayed," said Emily. "Such heart!"

"She was always so reassuring," Billy said. "She was a wonderful person to be with. Sometimes we would go for picnics along the beach. Every once in a while I'd steal a kiss."

He brought Emily to Charlotte to meet his family and to help him tell them that he had finally discovered his true calling: He was no longer in a quandary about his life's work. It was to be preaching. He felt they might find it amusing to learn that the decision had been made on the eighteenth hole of a golf course.

He described how it happened: "One autumn night, after a great deal of indecision, I walked out on the golf course that surrounds our school. I had practiced preaching, but believed my attempts were very feeble. I was in despair. On that night the trees were loaded with Spanish moss. In the moonlight it was a fairyland. As I stepped onto the fringe of the eighteenth green, I remember feeling that despite all appearances to the contrary, God did want me to preach. A soft breeze was sweeping from the south. I remember getting on my knees saying, 'Oh God, if you want me to preach, I will do it.' Tears ran down my cheeks. I made the surrender to become an ambassador for Jesus Christ."

Billy told his parents that he planned to ask Emily to be his wife and that jointly they would spread the Word. He was now convinced that he had an inspired purpose in life. The couple returned to school and continued to date regularly. Emily accompanied him as he preached the gospel at street corner meetings. Some Sundays he would hold seven or eight outdoor services from noon to dusk, often only to a handful of people. "No matter," he said. "All I ask is to stir one sinner."

Emily, however, began to have second thoughts about sharing Billy's life: "I had serious doubts. I attempted to tell him several times, but he would always put me off."

One evening at a school party she finally blurted it out—she had reconsidered his proposal of marriage. He tried to persuade her to change her mind. "At the time I couldn't believe it," Billy says. "I felt the world had ended for me. My confidence in myself was shattered. It took me a long while to make me realize that it was the best thing that's ever happened to me. I know now that God was preparing a girl for me in China!"

Ruth

Ruth's father, Dr. Nelson Bell, came from a fifth-generation Scottish-Irish Virginia family. For twenty-five years he served as a surgeon in a Presbyterian mission in China that was built by the father of author Pearl S. Buck. Once as the guest of honor at a White House dinner honoring "eminent humanitarians," Buck told the guests, "Of all the missionaries who ever went to China, Nelson Bell is the most hardworking and the most human."

A retired professor from the medical school that Bell

attended also spoke at the reception: "Nelson Bell was the most dedicated and gifted student I ever taught. From day one, he announced that he was going to be a medical missionary. He let nothing stand in his way. Eventually, he knew more than most of the instructors—myself included. When he got his medical degree in 1916 he had just turned twenty-one. I complimented him on his rapid achievement. 'That's to the good,' he replied. 'I'll have more time to be a medical missionary.' Four weeks later he and Virginia Leftwich, also from Virginia, were married."

Ruth's mother was equally committed. She took special nursing courses to assist her physician-husband. Shortly after their marriage they volunteered to serve in an impoverished West Virginia coal town. Fred Majewski, a retired miner who is now in his late seventies, remembers them well: "My father took me to see Dr. Bell after I had fallen out of a second-story window. Although everyone was sure that I was dying, the only damage was a broken arm. Mrs. Bell washed the blood off and Dr. Bell set the bone. Then he handed me a cherry-flavored lollypop. Candy was a real treat to poor kids in those days.

"Those two were darn good people—never demanded a single penny. Days later, my ma sent me over to their house with a blueberry pie she'd just baked. The door was open and I walked in. There were both of them kneeling on the floor, praying."

The Bells next journeyed overseas to a Presbyterian mission hospital in Tsingkiangpu, China, 300 miles north of Shanghai. It was usually well-stocked with supplies American church members shipped, but occasionally Nelson had to resort to assembling his own medical equipment. Even with the makeshifts, the lanky, erect doctor operated successfully on critically ill patients, many of whom had been given up for lost.

Nelson succeeded in treating a professional Mah-Jongg gambler who was suffering from a severe heart condition. Dr. Hsi Ch'ien, a Chinese doctor who was Bell's assistant, thought the man had only a few hours to live: "I've never seen a patient closer to death." It was in the thirties, long before pacemakers. Nelson constructed a pacemaker of his own, a contraption that kept the gambler alive for nearly a month.

Dr. Hsi said that in addition to prolonging the man's life, Bell also saved his soul. While patients were in recovery, the physician would talk to them in their regional dialects—he spoke five plus Mandarin—about the glories of Christ. His linguistic fluency was astonishing. Once during a meeting with Chiang Kai-shek, the Generalissimo told him, "Not only are you a doctor of miracles, but you speak Mandarin better than I do!"

Nelson refused credit for his deeds. "The work is solely His."

"He wasn't being coy," said Dr. Lorimer Davis, who had known Bell in China. "Nothing could shake his conviction that the Lord had given him the skill to help the unfortunates of Tsingkiangpu. He taught his children to think that way, too."

Billy Graham's future wife was born in Tsingkiangpu on June 20, 1920. It was a typical day: gunfire was heard in the distance, rats played around the town pump, bandits looted several shops, heavy rains flooded a nearby canal, and starving peasants envied the prosperous opium dealers.

The infant's mother believed that one's children came first, but she could often be found in the overcrowded wards or outpatient clinic. "We were always short-staffed," Virginia said. "I was needed to help out. It was difficult explaining it to my two very young children." (Rosa, an older daughter, had been born two years earlier.)

"Even as tiny youngsters," recalled Virginia, "they seemed to understand what I was saying. One minute they'd be crying. I'd tell them it was essential that I leave, and they'd stop their crying. Wang Nai Nai, our Chinese nurse-amah, used to say, 'Your children were kissed by the angels.' "

Ruth remembers her amah as one of the kindest people she's ever known. Wang Nai Nai had formerly been a procuress, who secured young girls for old men's pleasures. Her occupation changed radically when she heard a missionary speak about Jesus. "She really believed in the Master," said Bell. "Wang Nai Nai had truly been converted. It was such a joy to witness how each day she learned more and more about His love and mercy. I never saw anybody more deserving of admittance to the Church."

Rosa and Ruth were rarely out of their amah's sight. From early morning to late at night, the devoted Wang Nai Nai watched closely over them. The day always began with prayers and the singing of hymns, and it was a house rule that whoever came down to breakfast after the first verse of the hymn forfeited sugar on the porridge.

Nelson Bell felt the need for child-rearing directives. "Mrs. Bell and I strongly believe that structured family measures are necessary," he told John Hansberry, an American who worked in the office of the Consul-General in Shanghai. "Though children may grumble, we find they welcome guidelines. Without them, there would be total confusion."

For the two youngsters, the morning was school time. Virginia Bell tutored Rosa and Ruth because she feared they might be kidnapped if they attended a conventional grammar school. She instructed her daughters in the basic three Rs, gave them music lessons, taught them art appreciation and showed them how to knit and sew.

"Mother was a superb seamstress," Ruth said. "We never looked like refugees from a missionary barrel. She handmade most of our clothes. She believed that looking drab was a reflection on the Lord. She tried to pass her skill on to us, but we could never match her craftsmanship."

Virginia carefully studied the dresses in copies of *Harper's Bazaar* that were sent to her regularly by her sister-in-law, who lived in Waynesboro, Virginia. Then she copied them, adding her fine-needled embellishments. Although most of the garments were very plain, she had done such an outstanding job that it was rumored the Bells purchased Paris originals.

Shortly after the classes ended, Dr. Bell would join his family for lunch. Seated around the table, he would talk enthusiastically about his morning's surgery, becoming very graphic and giving vivid demonstrations.

After the noonday meal, Virginia and her husband would leave for the hospital, where in addition to her other chores, Virginia was in charge of the women's clinic. The girls, accompanied by Wang Nai Nai, would often discuss the future. Ruth, who has always had a serene faith in God, insisted that she, too, was going to be a devoted missionary. "She used to pray regularly that the Lord would allow her to become a martyr," Rosa recalled. "She so wanted to be captured by bandits and beheaded for Jesus' sake. Whenever she asked that, I would pray, 'Lord, please don't listen to her!' "

Each evening when Nelson and Virginia returned from the hospital, the family bathed and put on fresh clothes. "The clothing was not elaborate," said Ruth, "but we welcomed the change." After dinner, the Bell family gathered around the fireplace and played word games or read aloud. Ruth's favorite books of the Bells' large library were *Little Lord Fauntleroy*, *A Tale of Two Cities* and *David Copperfield*. Sometimes Nelson would entertain them with his guitar, followed by prayers and bedtime.

Ruth had a menagerie of beloved pets: pigeons, magpies, canaries, a baby turtle and a mongrel puppy named Tar Baby. She took excellent care of all the creatures but was especially partial to Tar Baby. She usually referred to the dog as T.B. "T.B. was a very odd-looking mixed breed," she said, "but to me she was the most beautiful dog in the world. I so loved her, but when she got older she started biting. Father had to put her down. T.B.'s death was my first real heartache. I don't think anything can be more intense than a child's grief."

Despite all the games and pets, life in Tsingkiangpu was very different from a conventional childhood in the United States. Although Ruth spoke Chinese before she learned English, in her environment she was inescapably an American, and thereby considered an oddity.

Her Chinese friends called her *yang kuei-tse*—foreign devil—and made frequent references to what they considered her big nose and huge feet. "I so wanted to be petite and look Chinese," Ruth recalled. "I would look in the mirror when washing and hope that my nose would shrink."

In the Bell home a daily battle was waged against dirt and germs. Virginia knew she had to keep the girls scrupulously clean to ward off vermin. Boiled water, yellow soap and baking soda were kept as handy as the family Bible. Mice were a constant nuisance; rats an ever-present terror. One night Virginia was awakened by screams coming from the girls' room. She dashed in and found rats crawling over their bodies. Ruth's right hand was covered with blood—a rat had bitten off a tiny corner of a finger.

Once while Ruth was playing in the mission garden, she noticed a small round metal object half buried in the soil and thought it was some kind of Christmas decoration. She picked it up, hung it on a nearby tree and admired it. Then, pleased with her fabulous find, she started to carry it into the house. Fortunately, a Chinese hospital worker who had recently been a soldier passed by. He recognized the "Christmas ornament" as a live grenade on its way to explode. Quickly he snatched the small bomb and tossed it into a bucket of water.

The routine on Sunday differed greatly from that of the rest of the week. Nelson and his wife believed that the sacred day belonged to the Lord. They didn't allow their children to engage in nonreligious activities—play outdoor games, read poetry or fiction or listen to secular music. "But don't get the idea," said Ruth, defending the practice, "that Sunday was dull or boring. Far from it. I was never forbidden to do one thing without mother or father providing a happy substitute. They made Sunday a special time, a day of refreshment, a gathering of strength. It was never dreary."

When Ruth was ready for secondary school, the Bells decided to send her to a Presbyterian-run academy in Pyongyang, North Korea. "It was a wrenching experience for me. The journey was a long one—it took a week to get there. I didn't want to go—adored my home. The idea of a classroom and competitive students terrified me. Night after night I cried myself to sleep."

Mary Edmondson, a classmate, said, "Homesick or not, she was an outstanding student; a bit lighthearted, but never without her well-thumbed Bible. She really knew its contents backwards and forwards—and fully believed. Yet she would express herself in a buoyant and easy manner. She had a crackerjack sense of humor. It kept getting her into trouble. I remember one time she was in the infirmary for the flu or some such. She was required to take her temperature several times a day and I guess she got bored. She put the thermometer under a light bulb that hung above her bed. When the nurse came to read the result she let out a shriek—it was 110 degrees!

"Another time Ruth was to be awarded some prize—it seemed like she was always winning something. Anyway, that morning we had room inspection. Just as the examining teacher was to give her stamp of approval, she heard a strange noise coming from under Ruth's bed. Upon closer inspection she discovered the noise was due to three tiny kittens. Ruth had placed them there when she found their mother had deserted them. I don't remember if, as punishment, the prize was withheld. But the next week she got into another fracas for which she was almost expelled. She crawled out of a window to make her exit. She was caught. What did she do? Reached for her Bible and prayed for guidance!"

Helen Torrey Renich also attended the Korean high school. "You knew instantly," she said, "that Ruth was a highly spiritual person. She was the first student I asked to join me in prayer. Later, four other girls joined our worship group. Every evening we would meet in my room to pray. I was so impressed by the way Ruth looked at the world. If it weren't for her devotion to God, I don't believe that Billy would be the evangelist he is today. I feel, looking at it from a woman's standpoint, that her walk with God was such that Billy always knew that his family was well cared for when he was away on his crusades. It gave him the strength he needed."

Ruth graduated near the top of her class. Again, in finding a college, the decision was to select a distant school. This time the choice was the United States, a place she had seen twice on family furloughs. The Bells picked Wheaton College, an interdenominational religious school twenty-five miles west of Chicago that their elder daughter was attending. It had an excellent academic reputation.

It was a tearful departure as the Bells saw their younger daughter off to America. Ruth, who has always enjoyed writing poetry, composed these lines during that lengthy ocean voyage:

> Test me, Lord, and give me strength
> to meet each test
>   unflinching, unafraid;

    not striving nervously to do my best
    not self-assured, or careless as in jest
            but with Your aid.
    Purge me, Lord, and give me grace
    to bear the heat
            of cleansing flame;
    not bitter at my lowly lot, but meet
    to bear my share of suffering and keep sweet
            in Jesus' Name.

"Wheaton sounded as alien to me as Peking University would seem to you," she said. "The little time I'd spent in America, my whole family was with me. It was going to be quite different now. Although my sister Rosa had preceded me to Wheaton, I was still mighty apprehensive. I wondered what lay in store for me."

Little did she realize that a tall, handsome, blond, wavy-haired student would soon cause her to pray, "Oh, Lord, if you wish to give me the privilege of sharing my life with this man, I would have no greater joy."

Nor could she know that, years later, this same man who so early caught her fancy would give thanks not only for his wife, but, uniquely perhaps, for his father-in-law. "I'm convinced," he said, "that one of the reasons in God's provisions why she became my wife was so Dr. Nelson Bell would become my father-in-law. He was by far the most unforgettable Christian I have ever known. . . . He and Ruth together did more to get my ministry church-oriented than any single factor and single influence."

2
MADE FOR
EACH OTHER

"GOD SELECTS AN ideal made for true worshipers," Billy said. "Of that I'm absolutely convinced. If you get impatient and refuse to wait for that choice, you wind up with His second- or third-best."

Whenever the evangelist makes this affirmation, he is asked, "How does one recognize God's choice?"

"It's difficult to explain to unbelievers or skeptics," he replies. "But the practicing Christian who really turns his life over to God's will recognizes the match at once. Everything else may be against it, but down deep inside you there is a difference. There is peace in your heart. You know this is the one; the one God wants you to have. It happened that way to me."

Billy became aware of God's selection almost from the first moment he saw Ruth Bell. "You can meet your life partner in a thousand different ways," he said. "In my case it was due to a rickety, yellow pickup truck."

Following graduation from the Florida Bible Institute, he enrolled in Wheaton College to study anthropology. At twenty-one years of age he was already an ordained minister. "But I strongly felt that I should have additional schooling," he said. "At Wheaton I needed money for expenses. I got a fifty-cents-an-hour job as a helper on a small moving truck. The owner, Johnny Streater, was a classmate of mine. He was always talking about an extraordinary coed named Ruth Bell. 'She's the prettiest girl on campus,' he would tell me, 'and also the most devout.' Naturally I was interested."

One afternoon, as Billy was about to unload an overstuffed living room chair, Johnny tapped him on the shoulder. "There's Ruth Bell I was telling you about," he whispered.

The future evangelist whirled around and saw an extremely attractive hazel-eyed girl who appeared to be in her late teens. "She was wearing a white dress," he said. "She looked like a vision. Immediately, I was in love again. But this time it was different from anything I had ever felt before. I was so flustered that I didn't make any sense in my greeting. I was told I uttered something that sounded like flub-glub."

The father of one of Ruth's girlfriends had told her about the slender young southerner who had recently enrolled in Wheaton. "He's quite different from all the other boys," he said. "Only twenty-one and already ordained. He's very intense in his love of God."

A few days later Ruth heard Billy pray. "I realized then that the description was accurate," she recalled. "It was in Wheaton's Williston Hall. A group of students held prayer meeting there before going out to teach Sunday school. I had never before heard anyone worship so devotedly. I immediately sensed that here was a young man who knew God in a very unusual way."

However, she wasn't fully aware of God's selection for her until after the first date with Billy. "Then it happened. When I got back to my room I remember thanking the Lord for allowing me to go out with Bill, who was unlike any other man I'd ever met. I always call him Bill. How could I possibly call a six-foot two-and-a-half-inch man Billy? He's never impressed me as being the 'Billy' type.

"There was a certain seriousness about him. There was a depth. Yet, for all his drive there was a winsomeness about him and a consideration for other people which I found very endearing."

That initial date came about a month after Streater's introduction. "I desperately wanted to see her again," Billy said, "but I guess I was too shy." He reasoned that he couldn't possibly impress this popular campus queen whose beauty and innocence had made her a school legend. Billy's friends realized how smitten he was and urged him to ask her out. Finally, after much coaxing, he timidly agreed to try. "It was in the school library," recalled Mary Blake, who was a Wheaton freshman at the time. "I was sitting next to Ruth. She was copying something out of a book. He started to walk over to our table. I remember being amused as I watched him make a half dozen stops and starts. He'd almost reach our table, then back off. Finally he seemed to stiffen up and stomped over.

"He opened his mouth, but nothing came out—it was as if he had suddenly lost his voice. But then he blurted, stringing the words together, 'Hey-Ruth-I'd-like-to-take-you-to-a-concert-next-Sunday-afternoon-how-about-it?' His face reddened right after he said it. I felt he was surely going to apologize for the interruption, but she looked up and smiled. 'Yes,' she answered. All he replied was, 'Thanks. Thanks a whole lot!' Then he waltzed out, as they say, on air."

Billy remembers that he found it very difficult to wait for Sunday! "I was never more impatient. Yet it was a combination of wanting the day to come immediately and hoping it would never roll around. I was so afraid I'd say or do the wrong thing."

Sunday did arrive, and Billy took Ruth to the concert. It consisted of sacred music. He did not disgrace himself. "Quite the contrary," Ruth said. "I found him very stimulating company. There was a decided purpose to his life which I thought admirable. That evening I was already wondering if I should share it with him."

On the walk back to her residence, the couple talked about what they hoped to contribute to the Lord. Billy thirsted to spread the Word in North Carolina; Ruth yearned to be a missionary in Tibet. Her wish to follow in her parents' footsteps presented a major obstacle to her growing feelings for Billy: "I had mixed emotions. On one hand I wanted to spend my life with Bill. But for years I had resolved to serve the Lord in Tibet. I reasoned that God got me here to Wheaton; He provided the money and helped me through my courses; weren't those certain signs that He was leading me straight back to the mission field?"

Billy knew that he was in love with Ruth, but he was terrified of saying so. He feared rejection—again. His declaration took place about two weeks after the concert. She remembers the incident: "We were out driving. Suddenly, right in the middle of a sentence, he jammed on the brakes. He did it so fast that we rammed right into the rear of a truck that had stopped for a red light. Luckily, no damage was done."

They continued to date. They would walk along the tree-shaded Wheaton streets, holding hands, sometimes in complete silence or heatedly engaged in discussions about Tibet.

"Why don't you go there with me?" she would ask.

"Because God wants me to preach right here," he would reply and quote biblical passages to aid his cause. "The Bible tells us 'It is not good that man should be alone; I will make him an helpmeet for him.' " He paused and then added, "If God caused me to fall in love with you, isn't it a clear sign that you're the helpmeet He has in mind?"

She'd look at him quizzically. "I'm praying hard for His guidance," she'd say.

Billy was certain that if Ruth did decide to marry, she'd choose him to be her husband. "Still," he said, "the reluctance to commit herself gave me a great deal of concern. Throughout the next year she tried to support her position by telling me stories of dedicated female missionaries. One of them was Mildred Cable, who rejected the man she loved in order to serve the Lord in China. Ruth also told me about Amy Carmichael, who cast aside her suitor so that she could dedicate herself to Indian children.

"I decided to let God do my courting. I wasn't above a little nudge. I'd ask her, 'Are you still praying about us?' Her reply was always the same: 'Yes. I'll tell you the moment He gives me an answer.' "

Mary Blake, the Wheaton classmate, recalls, "It seemed as if the entire school was aware of her confusion. We were all rooting for Billy. It was pretty obvious how they felt about each other. I don't know if real passion had yet struck. I'm told it came after they were married. But even then, those two had so much going for them—God and mutual respect. Maybe they're the most important ingredients for a successful marriage.

"However," she added, "there were some sharp differences. Mostly about religious doctrine. She was a Presbyterian—still is. Billy had joined the Southern Baptist Church. He gave as his reason that studying the Bible had convinced him immersion was the only proper form of baptism—and that Presbyterians didn't do it. He once said that Ruth's father couldn't possibly know the will of God because he was a Presbyterian. She was furious. He quickly apologized. I'm sure he never said that again.

"I'm told that Billy's theology has remained the same, but over the years his interpretation appears to be far more broadminded. He has clearly stated his views on differing denominations: 'All Christians hold essential convictions in common.' But during their courting there were some fireworks!"

Billy, who now was referred to as "the boy preacher," was often asked to deliver sermons at the Wheaton chapel. Ruth would sit in the front row, smiling, listening attentively. She admits that she was sometimes a little embarrassed by his frenzied bellowing and thrashing about of his long arms. (Billy speaks of his youthful zeal: "I listen to old tapes of myself and don't even know it's me. I bellowed and roamed all over the platform.")

News of his intense preaching fame spread to distant communities. During the summer vacation of his junior year he was invited to conduct a series of Gospel meetings in Tampa, Florida. Ruth was in Virginia with her missionary parents, who had been forced to leave China because of the Japanese invasion.

"I was still in a quandary regarding my future," she said. "I continued to ask the Lord for direction. Late one afternoon it became clear what His will was." She quickly posted a letter to Billy, who received it just as he was about to begin a Tampa revival meeting. He recalls that he fell to his knees in gratitude after reading: *"I'd be honored to become your wife."*

His father had given him a secondhand automobile, and in August 1941, he drove to see his bride-to-be. "Naturally," he said, "I was delighted to visit her. But I guess you couldn't tell it from my actions. I didn't kiss her on the lips. Instead, I merely pecked her on the forehead. I suppose I was self-conscious in the presence of her parents. Ruth has never forgotten that—she still kids me about it."

The first authentic betrothal kiss occurred a few evenings later. They were alone in the moonlight on a high mountain ridge. "It was a wonderful moment," Billy recalled. "But I was not as happy as I might have been: I didn't have enough money to buy her an engagement ring."

The opportunity arrived in early fall when the deacons of a church in his hometown asked him to lead them in a revival service. They were so pleased with the results that on the final evening they presented him with a special love offering of $165. The next morning he rushed to a jewelry store to purchase a small diamond ring.

In the fall Billy returned to Wheaton alone. Ruth had

decided to forgo a semester to tend her sister Rosa, who was convalescing from tuberculosis in a sanitarium in New Mexico. The affianced couple had to settle for carrying on their engagement via the post office, exchanging letters regularly. She told him in detail everything that was happening. He wrote to her about experiences at school. As the end of 1941 approached, he described the plight of the male students who were apprehensive about the impending war and how it would affect them.

When Pearl Harbor was bombed, Billy wanted to enlist immediately and be commissioned a chaplain. Army authorities told him that since Florida Bible Institute wasn't considered a seminary, he had to get a divinity degree from a recognized school or spend a year in a church pastorate.

Ruth and Billy's professors persuaded him to remain in college and graduate. Dr. V. Raymond Edman, the president of Wheaton, told him, "With more wisdom you can do your part in a much more meaningful fashion."

Billy's years at school were busy ones. After the doctors pronounced Rosa cured, Ruth returned to Wheaton. "It was good to see the change in Billy when she came back," Dr. Edman said. "He'd been moping about and was so absentminded." The engaged couple spent hours talking about how they planned to serve God together. They knew they would have to struggle not only with the physical destruction of World War II but with its heritage of bitterness and disillusionment.

Billy was now the regular pastor of the Wheaton Tabernacle Church, which served the students and faculty. Every Sunday he would preach twice to enthusiastic worshipers who crowded into the 300-seat auditorium. Ruth suggested topics for his sermons, and Billy sought her guidance in performing his duties as president of the Student Christian Council.

They graduated in June of 1943. Clutching his diploma, Billy whispered to his future wife, "Grow old along with me, the best is yet to be!"

3
THE PREACHER
TAKES A WIFE

BILLY AND RUTH were married two months later. They chose Friday the thirteenth for their wedding day. To a superstitious friend who expressed alarm over the supposedly unlucky selection, the about-to-be Mrs. Graham said, "I'm afraid I don't agree with your premonition of doom. To me it shall be the most wonderful day of my life."

Her happiness was very apparent on the ride to the church. "In order not to get her white satin bridal gown wrinkled," recalled her father, "Ruth stood up, bent over, on the back seat of the car all the way to the chapel, but she arrived flawlessly ironed. She kept repeating, 'It's a perfect wedding day, just as I dreamed and prayed it might be.' "

The ceremony was performed in the Southern Presbyterian Conference Center of Montreat, North Carolina, where the Bells now lived. The twenty-four-year-old bridegroom was uneasy about the guests' appraisal of him: "I was only known as the boy Ruth was about to marry. I remember their stares. I felt that they regarded me as a somewhat erratic person because I had switched my religious denomination. I stuck closely to my own clique."

Minutes after the "I pronounce you," the couple was engulfed in a shower of rice and headed for a brief honeymoon at Blowing Rock, North Carolina, an attractive village high in the Blue Ridge Mountains. Billy had selected an inexpensive boarding inn: He had $65 to spend.

"I could always recognize couples who had just had the knot tied," said Daniel Haywood, who worked as a part-time porter in a Blowing Rock hotel. "And it wasn't only because their shades were pulled all the way down—the Grahams' sure were! But from the shy, pleased smiles they had. A kind of rapture settled on the place when the Grahams were here."

When their money ran out after five days, the couple drove to Western Springs, Illinois, an upper middle-class suburb of Chicago. Billy, anxious to fulfill the Army's chaplain requirements, had accepted a position as the pastor of a small Baptist church that was badly in debt. "I had failed to inform Ruth about it before giving my consent," he said. "It was a big mistake. She was very hurt. Not that she objected to the church or the locale, but that I had failed to take her into my confidence. She felt strongly that a husband and wife should have the opportunity to discuss their responsibilities together. She ultimately forgave me, but I learned a valuable lesson. I believe that I have never since failed to consult her in an important decision."

The church building in Western Springs had never been

completed, compelling the thirty-five-member congregation to worship in the only room that was partly finished—the basement. It didn't have a proper ceiling, and a temporary tarpaper roof had been attached to the cement foundation; a sloping tunnel served as an entrance hall.

A parsonage—a place to live—didn't go along with the moldy, makeshift sanctuary, and Billy's $45-a-week salary wasn't sufficient to rent living quarters in affluent Western Springs. The couple had to settle for a tiny furnished apartment that was four miles from the pastorate.

"We got accustomed to bumping into each other," the evangelist said, "but we never really got used to the noise of the freight trains that thundered past our windows every hour."

To make the place appear more cozy-looking, Ruth attached a sheet of red cellophane to the living room wall. "We pretended it was a fireplace," she recalled. "Bill and I used to read in front of it. It was a blessing on cold Illinois nights."

Billy tried to help his wife. "But when it came to being handy," he says, "I don't think I succeeded too well. Ruth claims I can't drive a nail in straight. As a result she has had to learn to cope with most of the fixing. That's a real stumbling block in many marriages—the husband feels he has to prove his masculinity by doing all the home repairs although he knows his wife is far better at them."

A familiar sight in Western Springs was the young clergyman trotting to work. "Nowadays," he says, "people would think I was doing it for exercise, but at that time, I'm afraid that everyone in town knew it was because I didn't have enough money to spend on gasoline."

His path always took him past a high railway embankment. One day as he was brushing a falling cinder out of his eye he got an idea for a church-connected men's club. When he told the deacons about it, they tried to discourage him. They said that it couldn't possibly be successful because there were too few members. Ruth, however, felt it was a very worthy project. "It needs expanding," she said. "Start large." Together, she and Billy sent letters to politicians, physicians and scientists who lived within a fifty-mile radius of the church. They were invited to address the new men's club— which did not yet exist. Several accepted, and the Western Suburban Professional Men's Club was created. Soon, more than a hundred local men were attending the meetings.

Before long the church was too crowded, and meetings were held in a nearby restaurant. "Billy Graham knew how to fill the place," said Larry MacEwen, one of the waiters. "You better believe it. He had a dramatic kind of entrance. Guests would look for him in the front, but he'd enter at the back, take off his coat while he was still in the aisle. Once, he accidentally knocked a pitcher of water I was carrying. It spilled right onto the head of a big, fat Rotarian. Billy treated it just like a baptism. He said, 'God bless you!' and embraced the man. Instead of being sore, the guy just grinned. He was the loudest cheerer after Billy made a speech about the sacredness of holy matrimony. No marriage can survive, he claimed, if the partners live in completely different worlds."

Billy often tells a story to illustrate this point of view:

One day a hardworking North Carolina farmer asked his equally industrious wife to help him seed the corn. She agreed.

However, he soon bawled her out for flinging out the kernels too carelessly.

"Woman!" he yelled. "Don't waste my corn that way!"

"Your corn?" she replied. "It belongs to both of us."

"No!" he thundered. "This is my territory!"

Several hours later, when they returned to their frame farmhouse, the wife asked sweetly, "Fred, did you wipe your feet before going into the kitchen?"

"No, I didn't," he said.

"Well, you better do it right away! For this is *my* territory."

The Grahams' frugal budget was clearly the territory of both Ruth and Billy. They watched over it carefully. To help widen their outlook and purse, Billy accepted out-of-town preaching assignments. One Sunday morning as the evangelist was about to deliver his sermon in the First Baptist Church of Elyria, Ohio, an usher came up to the pulpit with his collection plate. This was a practice that Graham was unaccustomed to, and in his confusion he dropped in a $20 bill, thinking it was a single. At the end of the service he was about to admit his error, make a joke about it and grab his twenty back, which he badly needed for rent. But he overheard the ushers discussing the wealthy young minister's generosity. Reluctantly, he kept his silence.

Ruth, who was ill, had remained at home. Later, as he told her about the incident, she noted that her husband was very abashed. "Without you," he said to her, "I don't know how to manage unexpected things."

She laughed and replied, "In the eyes of the Lord, you'll not get credit for twenty dollars. One dollar was all you planned to give." She saw his expression turn from guilt to merriment.

Shortly after the $20 drop, their scrimped budget was helped by dinner invitations from members of the congregation. "They seemed to realize how badly we needed their kindness," Billy recalled. "I welcomed their hospitality. I have to admit I was slightly weary of the only cooking it seemed my bride knew how to prepare—Chinese! Chinese! All the time rice!"

4
EVEN
DEVOTED MATES
DISAGREE

LATE IN 1943, something special occurred in Billy's ministry: He was asked to take over a forty-five-minute Chicago evangelical radio program called "Songs in the Night." Dr. Torrey Johnson, a well-known midwestern Baptist pastor, had conducted the show, but had undertaken another church project and wanted Graham to become the new host. It required the signing of a thirteen-week contract and an outlay of several hundred dollars. Billy was assured that he could anticipate getting the money back through listeners' contributions.

His board of deacons thought the responsibility was much too great, but after a great deal of persuasion, they reluctantly agreed to let him give it a try. Ruth felt it was a splendid idea: "Bill accepted the challenge. There was lots of work involved, but its success let him reach multitudes outside the church. I knew that God had called him to minister to them and had given him the gift of communicating the Gospel to the unconverted."

She wrote the first script. Billy secured the services of George Beverly Shea, a popular baritone who has remained part of his evangelical team. The program, aired each Sunday evening, was an instant triumph. It continued to flourish long after Billy left it, the format the same. Listeners were still told that the show originated from "the friendly church in the pleasant community of Western Springs, Illinois."

"I've been a fan of it most of my adult life," said Reena Lowry, a native of Chicago. "I can still hear Bev Shea singing: 'And Can It Be That I Should Gain.' Billy called it one of his favorite hymns and said it represented his beliefs. He would urge listeners to make a decision for Christ. He'd do it in such a simple and compelling way that you immediately felt the Lord's presence. Billy often mentioned his wife on the air. One time, kidding, he said that she was a much better theologian than he was, even if she was a Presbyterian. He offered a reward to the person who could proselytize her for the Baptist church so that she could be baptized by immersion."

"Songs in the Night" was so successful that the young evangelist was invited to preach in Chicago's 3000-seat Orchestra Hall. The occasion was the initial meeting of a new group called Youth for Christ that had been founded by Dr. Torrey Johnson. Its purpose was to try to reach disillusioned young people who felt the future held no hope.

"That audience was the biggest I had ever seen," Billy

recalled. "I was gripped by the worst fit of stage fright of my life." Despite his fear, the sermon was well received. Johnson was so pleased that he asked Billy to make a series of addresses in Detroit, Philadelphia and Providence.

By now Billy had served a year as the Western Springs' pastor and had fulfilled the Army's requirements. He was accepted as a first lieutenant and told to await entry to the Harvard Divinity School for special training.

Returning from a Providence, Rhode Island, meeting of Youth for Christ, he seemed very flushed. A concerned Ruth took his temperature: 104 degrees. She summoned a doctor, who said that her husband had a severe case of mumps. "In a child it's usually not very serious," he told her. "But for a grown man it's far from a laughing matter."

For six weeks an extremely sick Graham was confined to bed. His fever fluctuated wildly and at one point Ruth feared that he was going to die. When he was permitted to walk around, he attempted to go back to work, but his voice was so weak that an anonymous listener of his radio program sent him $100 so he could "recuperate in sunny Florida."

Due to the ailment a very heavyhearted Billy was discharged from the Army. "How strange and mysterious are God's ways in our lives," he now says. "I felt miserable about being drummed out. It was Ruth who convinced me that I could reach many more servicemen and accomplish my ministry a great deal more effectively than if I went into the chaplaincy. But at the time I did a great deal of bitter disagreeing and wasn't the easiest husband in the world to live with."

"He wasn't," Ruth agreed. "But I have never expected or

wanted married life to be free of arguments. Just before I became a bride, a very wise woman told me that when couples have exactly the same thoughts on everything, one of them is unnecessary."

In the early days of their marriage, the Grahams held many opposite viewpoints. Some of the dissent was of a major nature, such as Billy's taking a church and departing from full-time evangelism. Others were insignificant, but also gave cause for pain and agitation. Ruth had to endure her husband's half of the closet always being in a mess and his constantly using the top of the bathroom door as a towel rack. They differed on what constituted desk-neatness and on Billy's fancy of wearing gaudy, hand-painted ties.

"Granted," he says, "most of them were small things. But, then, minor-appearing disagreements can cause some of the biggest arguments. Just think for a moment about the issues that you find disturbing.

"I had yet," he added, "to learn that young husbands and wives have a difficult time adjusting to their new life and to each other. I admit that occasionally I felt sorry for myself and wondered if habitual debating was what the future would hold. Fortunately, that feeling didn't last very long. However, judging from the mail I receive, for some couples it seems to go on for years and years."

Ruth has met wives who believe that a Christian marriage means submission in all things, regardless of the wife's better judgment. She has observed that in cases where this has been tried, both partners are badly hurt. "It makes the husband believe that wrong is right," she says. "He begins bragging how wise he is and starts feeling superior to his wife. She in turn becomes increasingly resentful. Although she may try not to show her displeasure, it becomes apparent in dozens of ways, from domestic lapses—burned stew, unmatched socks—to sexual coldness.

"However," Ruth adds, "it is a good thing to know when and how to disagree. It's possible to disagree without being disagreeable." She offers a few valuable suggestions adopted from her own experience:

1. Be sure you know what the issue is, then ask yourself if it's worth disagreeing about.
2. When arguing, carefully examine the tone of your voice—make sure it isn't too loud and you aren't talking out of turn, or interrupting.
3. Don't inject snide personal remarks.
4. Don't suddenly go off on a tangent and start introducing unrelated subjects.
5. Stick to the facts—don't embroider or exaggerate. If the facts won't carry you, you ought not to be arguing at all.
6. If you win or lose—do it graciously.
7. If you can't come to a friendly agreement—win, lose or compromise—lay it down for a while. Let it rest. Have faith that things will change, for they surely will. Postpone arguing if you're still sizzling with anger. Don't use tears to make your husband knuckle under.

Ruth remembers the first quarrel she had with Billy: "Just after we were married, he and some of his bachelor friends decided to drive to Chicago. I asked if I might go along to do some window-shopping. In those days that was all we could afford. 'No!' Bill snapped. 'This trip is for men only!' As I saw the car draw away I kneeled down in front of our living room couch and prayed, 'Lord, if you'll forgive me for marrying him, I promise I'll never do it again.'

"Later, when Bill returned, he apologized for being so thoughtless. I told him about my fatuous prayer. We chuckled as we held hands—a sense of humor sure helps those who disagree."

Billy felt it was far from a laughing matter when he told his wife about a job offer he had received to be a paid representative of Youth for Christ.

"I don't think I should accept it," he said. "The plan is to organize in every city—it would mean being away from you for weeks at a time."

"A wife has to know how her husband really feels," Ruth said. "I realized how strongly he felt about evangelism." She took his hand, and together they knelt and prayed for guidance. He gave up the Western Springs pastorate and took the Youth for Christ position.

Because Ruth was expecting their first child, it was decided that she would temporarily move in with her parents in Montreat. The interim arrangement became permanent. For three years the Graham home was in a Bell second-floor bedroom. Between crisscrossing the United States and Canada, Billy managed to spend brief moments with his wife and new daughter, Virginia, who was born on September 21, 1945, as he rushed home from Mobile, Alabama.

"Billy drove himself pitilessly," said Torrey Johnson, the Youth for Christ founder. "He always seemed to be in a hurry to serve the Lord. Yet he worried that he couldn't find more time to spend with his family. I remember several months after Virginia was born he appeared conscience-stricken as he showed me a photograph of her. 'Wouldn't it be ironic,' he said, 'if she desperately needs her father while he's out saving other children?' Then he put the picture away and returned to the case at hand: How best to attract youth to Christ? He sure had some bright ideas."

Magicians, ventriloquists and cheerleaders were used. In Minneapolis, Billy once borrowed one hundred pianos for a gala revival concert. He explained his florid methods: "We employed every modern means to catch the attention of the unconverted. And then we punched them right between the eyes with the Gospel."

Munroe Erbsen, who now drives a taxi in a Minneapolis suburb, was a fifteen-year-old dropout when he attended the rally. "I went because the advertisement of all those pianos sounded positively bananas. They sure made a lot of noise, but they were whispers compared to Graham. I had never seen him before and expected some little white pipsqueak. Here was this tall, good-looking guy—tough-looking, too, especially when he talked about Jesus.

"I was there with a couple of the fellows. I thought we'd be the only blacks, but there were a few others. That was surprising because I had heard 'Youth for Christ' was definitely anti-black. Some of them started to razz Graham. Me, too. But I soon stopped. He really got to me when he started speaking about racial tension. He said that one of the most urgent tasks of a Christian was to overcome personal prejudice and hate. He sounded like he really meant it. I found myself believing him when he told us that following Christ was the only answer. When it came time to march down the

60

aisle and declare yourself for the Lord, I did.

"Billy took a good position on integration long before the Supreme Court decision. I was told that once in Dallas he went to a lily-white hotel elevator accompanied by a black friend. The operator refused to take the black man up and ordered him to use the rear stairs. This made Billy real mad and he yelled for the manager. 'Either he rides with me or we both use the rear stairs!' The manager was afraid of offending the famous preacher. He gave in quickly. Billy and his black friend rode up. I heard that Billy got a lot of cursing letters from the Ku Klux Klan because of his racial ideas. If you ask me, he's a very decent sort." (Names of many of the people Billy helped convert have been changed.)

The lavish compliments became somewhat subdued as twenty-eight-year-old Graham temporarily left the limelight to head three religious institutions in Minnesota called the Northwestern Schools. They consisted of an interdenominational Bible Training Institute, a seminary, and a college of liberal arts. At first Billy refused the switch to academia. Ruth strongly counseled against his making the move. However, eighty-six-year-old Dr. William Riley, the founder of Northwestern Schools, was persistent. A former evangelist himself, he had heard Billy preach and was convinced he would be the ideal successor.

"I was summoned to Dr. Riley's bedside during a heavy rainstorm," Billy recalled. "I'll never forget the darkness of his room, broken only by the flashing of lightning and a bony finger pointing at me. 'For years I've run this place,' Dr. Riley gasped. 'Now it's your turn. God has willed it so. I'm leaving it to you as Elijah gave his mantle to Elisha. As Saul appointed David, King of Israel. You'll be disobeying God if you refuse.' "

Billy continued to protest, but now admits feeling exhilarated by the idea of being hand-picked as heir to a minister whom William Jennings Bryan once called "The greatest Christian statesman in the American pulpit."

He told Dr. Riley that he would accept the presidency of the schools on an interim basis.

Ruth, who was expecting their second child, remained in Montreat. According to Dr. Bell, "At the time, my son-in-law seemed to be the busiest person in the world. Not only was he now responsible for an 850-member student body, but he was still the vice-president of Youth for Christ. He tried to get home as often as possible, but it wasn't easy. With an expanding family, he and Ruth secured a $4000 mortgage and bought a small house across the road from us."

Dr. Bell recalled that early in May of 1948 he phoned the evangelist to come immediately, for Ruth was in labor. "He managed to board a plane right after my call. He took a taxi from the airport and rushed to the hospital, carrying a bouquet of flowers. As he marked time in the waiting room, he fell asleep. I had to shake him awake to announce, 'You're the father of a baby girl. Your wife is doing fine.' "

It was about this time that Billy became solemnly bothered by doubt: "Not about the deity of Jesus Christ, not about the Gospel of His preaching, but concerning the authenticity, authority and inspiration of some of the Scriptures. I wondered if the Bible could be trusted completely. A close friend of mine had experienced a change of heart and mind toward the Scriptures. He was a successful minister of my age. We had many long discussions. He was forever pointing out contradictions. He was one miserable man. Now, so was I."

After a six-months struggle, Graham did something he advises for all 'doubting Thomases': "I had forgotten that when you have a serious problem, there is a wonderful, certain way to solve it. I fell on my knees and asked the Lord for guidance. I prayed a long time. I asked Him if I was wrong. If His Word was true.

"Suddenly I sensed the presence and the power of God as I had not felt Him for a long time. I was confirmed in my total faith and trust. Doubt left me. And I knew that I had passed an important crisis in my ministry."

5
MY CUP
RUNNETH OVER

AN OLD FRONTIER tale concerns Hector Baylor Jenkins, M.D., who practiced his healing art in the Texas panhandle during the late 1800s. Not only was Dr. Jenkins a very industrious physician, but he also served as the hardworking town marshal, mayor, school principal and undertaker. For miles around his grateful constituency exclaimed: "That Hector sure is dedicated!"

Mrs. Sadie Jenkins, Hector's uncomplaining wife of thirty years, agreed. "My cup runneth over," she said. Then added stoically, "And over and over."

"Occasionally," Ruth Graham recalled, "I felt exactly the same way. I suppose at times every wife does. Some complain of their husband's devotion to his job, or of being a golf widow. Husbands frequently gripe about the children and the housecleaning having first priority. In my marriage it was sharing Bill with his call to the Lord. From the outset I was committed to it, but his being a college president wasn't exactly the direction I'd had in mind."

Billy soon realized that his wife was right in urging him to spread the word of God. He found himself devoting fewer and fewer hours to the Northwestern Schools as he delegated academic responsibilities to assistants. Gradually he resumed the hectic life of the full-time evangelist.

"We could plainly see it happening," said Dr. O. E. Sandsen, dean of the liberal arts college. "It became pretty obvious that Billy Graham's heart and soul belonged to making people accept the Lord Jesus Christ. He frantically wanted to bring the Gospel to as many as possible."

In the 1948-49 season, Billy accepted crusade invitations to a half dozen small-and medium-sized cities. Repeatedly, he told audiences that marriage was sacred. "But you'd never know it from what you read in the newspapers!" he thundered. "When a Hollywood movie star weds for the third or fourth time, column after column glorifies the new union. You're made to think that a single marriage is old-fashioned and that modern living calls for a wide variety of mates. . . . What can you do? Right now you can turn to Jesus!"

Graham's first major crusade was in Los Angeles. He told Ruth he was worried about reaching so many people. She tried to convince him that he'd do just fine. Still, he expressed doubts. Her usual practice had been not to accompany him to out-of-town campaigns. They had agreed that her role was to stay at home and care for the children. This time, however, he seemed so disconsolate that she decided to join him.

"Her having faith in me helped tremendously," he said. "Over the years I've discovered how vital it is to have your marriage partner believe in you; not to keep saying, 'You're sure to fail!' Too often, a spouse down plays you so much that you begin thinking, 'That's what really caused my defeat!' The result is two estranged mates."

Spot radio announcements heralded the sensational young evangelist and his dazzling array of Gospel talent. Billboards showed a clergyman spreading butter on a slice of bread. The caption read: IT'S A SIN TO SPREAD IT SO THIN. COME TO THE BILLY GRAHAM RALLY AT THE LARGEST TENT IN THE WORLD! Posters advertising the TWENTY-TWO TREMENDOUS NIGHTS IN THE CANVAS CATHEDRAL were plastered throughout Los Angeles.

William Randolph Hearst heard about Billy's mission and issued strict orders to his editors: "Puff Graham!" They did, and dozens of stories glamorizing the "amazing young evangelist who is saving us from the devil" started appearing.

Billy says that he had never talked to or communicated with Hearst. "But I've always believed," he told reporters, "that if anybody wants to extol Jesus Christ, it would be sinful to object."

Henry Luce, founder of Time-Life, also impressed by Billy Graham, followed Hearst's lead. Both of Luce's magazines carried stories about the crusade. After being introduced to Billy by Bernard Baruch, he told the financier, "He is indeed the Pied Piper of revivalism. I predict that very soon his converts will sharply multiply. They'll number in the thousands."

The Los Angeles crusade had been scheduled to last a month. The sponsors were so pleased they decided to extend it. For eight weeks, the tall, handsome evangelist clipped a tiny microphone to his necktie and rapidly strode to the pulpit of the gigantic tent, which had been enlarged to accommodate 9000 people. Despite the additional seats, there was nearly always standing room only. He'd pause, stare straight ahead, open the top button of his shirt, raise his long arms and start preaching with a desperate urgency.

He never spared his audience from what he thought the truth to be. "Christianity isn't easy," he'd say as his fists clutched the air. They listened anxiously as he told them, "All of you, at one time or another, have violated the Ten Commandments. 'Slightly,' you say. But in the sight of God, there is no such thing as a slight sin." He'd suddenly close his eyes and bow his head; then he'd jerk up straight as he lashed out. " 'Thou shalt not murder,' we're told. You claim that surely doesn't apply to you. 'Why, I even go to church on Sunday!' you protest. Well, I have news. There are thousands of husbands and wives in this city—some sitting right here—who are killing their marriage partners by neglect. Yes, you are guilty of murder!"

A smaller tent—500 seats—was used for prayer and counseling sessions. It was staffed by volunteers and open twenty-four hours a day. Ruth Graham was one of the advisers who talked daily to prostitutes, pimps and alcoholics. One streetwalker remembers her as being an excellent listener. "For maybe twenty minutes or longer she just let me do all the talking. She seemed to sense how badly I wanted to spill my guts."

Jim Vaus was one of the 350,000 who visited Billy's tent. Vaus, the son of a Baptist minister, had tossed religion aside and drifted into crime. He had been jailed twice. Currently, he was in the employ of Mickey Cohen, who was known as the czar of the Los Angeles underworld. Vaus' speciality was wiretapping racetracks and bordellos.

"One day my wife, Alice, and I were just driving around," Vaus recalled. " 'Why don't we pay a call on this Graham fellow who's been getting all this publicity,' I said to her. 'It ought to be good for a lot of laughs.' "

They found seats near the back of the tent just as Billy boomed, "There's a man in this audience who has heard this story many times before, and who knows this is the decision he should make. . . . This may be his last opportunity!"

"It startled me," Vaus said. "I was convinced he had singled me out. I pretended not to hear. But a few minutes later he repeated, 'This may be your last opportunity—your moment of decision!' I couldn't keep still any longer. I shouted, 'I'll go! I'll go!' "

John Pollock, Billy Graham's official biographer, said, "Vaus was one of the more sensational converts. Much has been written about the gangster turning to God. However, Billy feels that the writers have overlooked one of the most moving and wonderful results of the transformation—the rebirth of the Vaus marriage. He says that it quickly turned from hopelessness to jubilation. One of the things that pleased Billy best about the Los Angeles crusade was that many divorced couples, or near divorced, came to hear him preach. There, right in the tent, they decided to reunite."

Another convert was a former American medal winner at the 1936 Berlin Olympics. Louis Zamperini was not only a champion long-distance runner, but had electrified spectators by pulling down a Nazi swastika flag. During World War II he survived forty-seven days on a liferaft and thirty months in a

Japanese prison camp. Back home, the authentic athlete-soldier hero was toasted by some of the country's leading citizens, including the President of the United States. He was given a ticker-tape parade. However, Zamperini's fame quickly vanished and he turned to alcohol.

"I hit rock bottom," he said. "I was lower than low. That's when I attended the Graham revival meetings in Los Angeles. I was pretty hostile at first, but I kept coming back. I will be forever thankful that I did. It changed my life. For the first time I felt peace in my heart."

6
"MAY THE LORD
BLESS YOU REAL GOOD"

IN THE FALL of 1950, Billy was asked to lead a weekly radio revival service to be known as "The Billy Graham Hour." At first he rejected the suggestion, saying it would be too time consuming.

Ruth, who has always believed that true evangelism practiced on radio or television would attract many converts, liked the idea and offered to help. However, she felt the name might be considered in poor taste. Instead, she proposed calling it "Hour of Decision."

By now, Billy had learned the value of his wife's advice and agreed to try her suggestion for thirteen weeks. The program, with Ruth's title, made its debut several months later on fifty-two ABC outlets. He wound up the initial session with a signature that became his trademark: "May the Lord bless you real good."

Soon, 800 ABC stations, coast to coast, carried the show.

A Gallup poll revealed that it had become the most popular religious program ever to be aired. It was estimated that more than 15 million listeners heard it regularly. Billy's radio sermons often included his favorite Bible verses:

Luke 12:15
And he said unto them, Take heed, and beware of covetousness: for a man's life consisteth not in the abundance of the things which he possesseth.

"This verse indicates," Billy said, "that our lives are far more than materialism. That's why so many people in the affluent western world are disillusioned. Our obsession with materialistic things has brought about a great sense of emptiness and boredom. I often quote this passage and similar ones to myself so that I do not get absorbed with the materialism of our age. There are other deeper spiritual and moral things that are much more important to building character and preparing one for eternity."

I Corinthians 10:13
There hath no temptation taken you but such as is common to man: but God is faithful, who will not suffer you to be tempted above that ye are able; but will with the temptation also make a way to escape, that ye may be able to bear it.

"Often when I have faced trial and temptation, I have quoted this verse to myself. It has been a great encouragement and comfort to me. It indicates that when temptation comes, God always provides a way to escape. The Scriptures indicate that we are tempted daily, thus a verse like this memorized can provide great comfort and might to the Christian."

Philippians 4:13
I can do all things through Christ which strengthenth me.

"When the challenge is too great or I become bone weary in the midst of a long crusade or I become discouraged, I find solace in this passage. Concerning the great prophet Elijah, the Scripture says he was 'a man of like passions.' So am I. I need the encouragement of God's word daily."

Matthew 25:35-36
For I was an hungred, and ye gave me meat: I was thirsty, and ye gave me drink: I was a stranger, and ye took me in: Naked, and ye clothed me: I was sick, and ye visited me: I was in prison, and ye came unto me.

"This verse makes me remember that I have a responsibility to the poor and friendless. Nothing expresses that responsibility better than this passage."

John 3:16
For God so loved the world, that He gave His only begotten Son, that whosoever believeth in Him should not perish, but have everlasting life.

"These twenty-five words actually compose the entire Gospel. John 3:16 is a Bible in miniature. It is the very essence and heart of what I believe and preach."

Proverbs 3:11
My son, despise not the chastening of the Lord; neither be weary
of his correction.

"It has been my experience that when I get off track, God
has a way of spanking me and putting me back on the straight
and narrow. He has had to chastise me many times in my life.
His discipline has hurt, but it has been good for me. I know
He has always done it from a heart of love."

Proverbs 3:5
Trust in the Lord with all thine heart; and lean not unto thine
own understanding.

"I suppose over the years I have quoted this passage
several thousand times. And each time I feel it intensifies in
rightness."

Proverbs 3:6
In all thy ways acknowledge Him, and He shall direct thy paths.

"My mother gave me this verse as a Christmas present
when I was nine years old. She insisted that I memorize these
words so they could live in my mind forever. That verse has
been a staff and strength in my life. What little I may be, I am
because of them."

In addition to conducting the radio program, Billy began
writing a widely read newspaper column called "My Answer,"
which was syndicated in seventy-five newspapers. Many of
those surveyed in the Gallup poll reported they read it daily

and had also purchased the evangelist's book, *Peace with God*, which appeared on best-seller lists, sold more than a million English copies and several million more in foreign translation.

"I wrote it because of my conviction that a book was badly needed that would present the Gospel in utter simplicity," Graham explained.

Myrna and Bradley Henderson, II, are two of his most enthusiastic advocates, won by that plain matter-of-factness. "We belie the notion that all Billy Graham converts are hard-hats or go around in undershirts," Bradley Henderson said. "I was a Rhodes Scholar and have a doctorate in jurisprudence," he adds proudly. "Myrna majored in sociology and anthropology. We met at a chamber music get-together. I play the violin. She, the cello. We both like French wine, bird watching and Quiche Lorraine. We even rang doorbells for Adlai Stevenson when he ran for President. So I don't think we can be dismissed as a pair of Bible Belt followers.

"It was at a chamber music rehearsal at Jeff Miller's house that Billy Graham's name was first brought up. Midway through Bach's Sinfonia Number 3 in D, I tossed my bow down and started yelling at Myrna. 'Can't you read music? It's supposed to be cheerful. You're playing it like a dirge. You're at least five beats behind! Cooperate, you nincompoop!"

" 'You're the nincompoop!' she yelled back. 'You're sick! Sick! Sick!' Then she stamped out, not even bothering to take her cello.

"We were always fighting—not just about music. It seemed that the squabbling went on from the moment we opened our eyes until we wearily dropped off to sleep. Even that wasn't immune from fighting. Sometimes Myrna would wake me to bitterly complain that I had opened the windows too wide or that I had failed to turn up the electric blanket.

"It seemed that we disagreed about everything. About our sex life. About the meals. About the proper way of raising children—we have twin daughters who are now in their early twenties. Darn little was exempt.

"I was at the end of my rope as where to turn or what to do. We had tried marriage counselors, encounter groups, transcendental meditation. We even contemplated mate swapping. We talked about divorce and had separated half a dozen times. We always came back because of the children. I had become resigned to a lifetime of fighting. I was convinced that it would only end when one of us was carried out in a mahogany casket.

"It was right after the Bach fiasco that Jeff Miller gave me a paperback copy of *Billy Graham Answers Your Questions*. The book contained some of the replies the evangelist made in his newspaper column. 'This guy has very sound judgment,' Jeff said. 'It might help.'

"Jeff is a senior partner in the law firm I work for. He's very astute and clients pay heavily for his advice. He works very hard. I always felt that he was the most coolheaded of men. He could see how skeptical I was.

" 'Don't let the fact that he's a celebrity fool you,' Jeff said. 'Read the book! Try to pretend that it's research for a lawsuit you're appealing.' To be polite, I put Graham's book in my briefcase.

"When I got home, Myrna was showing the girls how to

make fudge. I was given the silent treatment. I didn't much care. Actually, I welcomed it, as it would give me a chance to study some papers I brought home from the office. As I unzipped my case, I noticed the book Jeff had given me. Because I respected him, I thumbed through it.

"I suppose it would make a sensational story if I claimed that I saw the light instantly. And from that moment on my marriage became super-dandy. Well, it didn't happen that way. I'll plead guilty that I found some of the answers provocative, but as a practicing attorney I was prepared to offer a rebuttal. I put the book away. The next morning the Henderson eternal state of war resumed.

"When I got to the office on Monday, I ran into Jeff Miller. He didn't ask me if I had liked the book. That's not his way. I felt that he was waiting for me to offer the first word. He kept looking at me quizzically the rest of the week. I was glad when Friday arrived.

"The next morning Myrna took the girls to the orthodontist. I puttered around in the garden and in my den. The book was on the desk. I picked it up. This time I read it from cover to cover.

"I'm not superstitious, but something happened while I was holding the book. For no reason at all, it suddenly fell to the carpet, landing faceup to this passage:

Q: I expected my marriage to be beautiful and sublime, but it has turned out to be the reverse. . . . Do you think Christ could help me?

A. A family home is intended to be a haven of rest in a world of unrest. And with Christ in the home it can be a refuge from life's storms. Members of a household may be selfish. Our likes

76

and dislikes are not always the same. Tensions are set up and discord follows. Christ has the power to bring peace for He strikes at the center of selfishness. He makes us considerate of others. In His presence, home becomes a place where sharing is an ethic and peace a reality. This is not to say that there is never any discord in a Christian home. But that discord is shortlived and the goal is harmony instead of self-fulfillment.

"I suppose I was 'born again' before it became fashionable," Henderson continued. "Nothing grandiose in its occurrence. An Episcopal clergyman simply welcomed me back. I didn't try to proselytize Myrna. But at times she acted as if she was impressed by what getting religion had done for me. I had learned a very valuable lesson—it takes two to engage in an argument. I stopped rising to her bait. Finally she got tired of provoking me. But it did take almost two years before she was ready to step forward."

Myrna Henderson is the direct opposite of her husband. Whereas he is fragile-looking, she is quite robust. "Her 135 pounds are well distributed," Bradley Henderson said. "Occasionally, our fighting reached the beating-up stage. I must admit she was always the victor."

"It became so obvious," Myrna said, "that some of our friends began calling me 'Myrna, the Goddess of Mars.' At the time I sort of liked the title. However, I do prefer the present one: 'Myrna, the Muse of Mercy.'

"There's a saying about children being impressionable. It's so true. The twins were the first to notice what religion was doing for their father. They asked if they might go along with him to church. I don't mind admitting that I was plenty peeved. Brad and I always had a definite understanding about the children and religion. We agreed that we would never try to influence them.

"In no uncertain words I reminded him of that commitment. I suppose I stormed and ranted. In his new reasonable way, he calmly told me that it was their own decision. Despite my resentment, I soon realized that he was right—it was solely their own will.

"It probably sounds like a hodgepodge of banality, but I credit our daughters with being the ones that led me to God. I've always described myself as being extremely close to them. The very thought of being an outsider was more than I could stand. Some of my friends felt that I had suddenly become deranged. They'd tell me, 'It was bad enough when Brad did it, but you? We always credited you for having more sense. Can't you see that this Billy Graham character is nothing more than a modern Billy Sunday? That his soft and easy path to heaven is just a camouflaged sawdust trail?'

"They went on and on like that, saving their knockout blow for the very last. 'Wise up, kid,' they'd say. 'Life isn't the simple and sentimental relationship between man and God he speaks of. It isn't that easy! To live in this world you've got to be practical.'

"Dr. Graham's simplicity is what Brad and I admire most. We don't think it's that complicated to realize that we all need someone to cling to. Someone to make life worthwhile. Dr. Graham told us what that someone was. Oh, I know his Ph.D. is honorary. So what? If he had sufficient time I'll wager he could earn a dozen academic titles. I was delighted to learn that he has a degree in anthropology. That was one of my majors in college and I know how valuable the subject is in today's world. I believe that my professors would agree with many of the answers he gave in his book:"

Q: Can having faith in God save our home and turn it into a happy place to dwell?

A: Yes! A home is like a solar system. The thing which holds the solar system together is the fact that a great sun is its center. If it were not for the sun, our solar system would fly to pieces. Well, unless the Son of the living God, the Lord Jesus Christ, is put at the center of your home, it too will fly to pieces.

7
MISSION: TO SAVE
MERRY OLDE ENGLAND

GRAHAM'S FIRST INTERNATIONAL triumph, the spectacularly successful Greater London Crusade, came in 1954. It was sponsored by clergymen from more than a thousand local Protestant churches. They were concerned about diminishing congregations in the post-World War II period, and turned to Billy hopefully.

Despite their confidence in the American evangelist, overwhelming defeat was threatened in the outset. As soon as his ship, the *United States,* docked at Southhampton, he received a rigorous roasting from the English fourth estate. Ruth, who had decided to accompany him to offer support, wasn't spared. Just before the first press conference began, he asked her to remove her lipstick. It didn't help.

One of the early questions was directed to her. "Is it true that your husband carries around his own special bottle of baptism water?" a reporter asked. As she thought of the appropriate negative reply, another journalist snapped, "Who invited you over here, anyway?"

That evening, London newspapers carried dozens of anti-Graham stories. Typical was the one which appeared in a Fleet Street tabloid: "In America, John the Baptist's name has been changed to Billy. Armed with Bible-sixgun and sombrero-halo he buckles down to his self-appointed mission: snatching sinners from the jaws of hell. Now, he comes to our shores to save Merry Olde England. And Billy Boy claims he's the bloke to do it!"

The People, a weekend gazette with a huge circulation, also lambasted "Silly Billy." Their chief reporter wrote: "Must we be turned better citizens and kinder husbands by the antics of Billy's American hot Gospel circus?" Even the sedate and venerable *Times* speculated, "Is the American revivalist overextending himself?"

Graham had started assembling a team of topflight evangelists to help him spread the Gospel. They urged him to refute all the negative stories. He was unwilling. "I'm not going to answer mudslinging with mudslinging."

The team had rented Haringey Arena, a cavernous hall that was used for boxing matches and greyhound racing. Colorful placards heralding the three-month-long crusade were plastered all over town. United States Senators Stuart Symington and Styles Bridges, who were visiting England at the time, issued press statements stating they would be present at the opening session.

Late in the afternoon, Symington phoned to extend his apologies: "I'm afraid that Styles and I can't make it. An important meeting has just come up." Billy told Ruth it was obvious that the Senators were bowing out because of all the adverse criticism.

As the evangelist and his wife were preparing to leave for the nearby arena, an aide called to tell them it was only a fifth full and that newspaper photographers were snapping pictures of all the empty seats.

"If a devoted mate was ever necessary," Billy recalled, "this was the time. I was a sorry case of nerves. I kept thinking how miserably I had failed. Ruth gave me the sense of confidence I so badly needed. She reminded me that people all over the world were praying for us. That whatever the circumstance of the evening, God would be glorified. I believe that more husbands and wives fail through discouragement than for any other reason."

The Grahams made the short drive to Haringey, which because of heavy traffic took almost half an hour. Holding hands, they entered the lobby—it was deserted. Suddenly a member of the Team rushed up. "It's a miracle!" he shouted excitedly. "Inside, the arena is jammed. Every seat is taken and thousands are standing in the street on the other side of the building!"

He escorted them to a small office. Both Senators were there. As Bridges kissed Ruth's cheek, Symington said, "We're supposed to be having dinner with Anthony Eden, the foreign minister, but we decided we couldn't let you down."

"It turned out to be one of the most glorious nights of my life," Billy said. As he delivered his message, "Does God Matter?", one of the women in the audience shouted, "Billy, you reminded us that He does! God bless you!"

When Billy wound up his sermon, 178 men and women of

all ages marched down the aisles to make their decision. One of them, Charles Parker, a chemist who worked in a Piccadilly pharmacy, told the London *Daily Mirror,* "I suppose you'd call my marriage an acceptable one. Meredith and I rarely clashed—we certainly didn't lead a dog-and-cat existence. Oh, I'm not going to pretend that we had a wildly amorous relationship. We were too self-centered for that. You might say that we suffered from 'waxy tongues of vanity.'

"It was Graham who made me recognize that I was the possessor of a bad case of selfishness. And that selfishness was one of the greatest problems a marriage had to endure. He claimed that when you accepted Christ, the selfishness disappeared, as you now were able to submit your ego to Him. And that's exactly how it happened to me."

Since the crusade meetings were usually held at night, Billy often spoke at schools and hospitals during the daytime. He had been invited to address the students at the London School of Economics. As he was being introduced, one of the professors stood up and in a booming voice bellowed, "This is the first time a clergyman has been allowed to accost us! I object strenuously! I was under the impression that this was a secular school!" The students roared their approval.

Billy smiled and started his talk. Suddenly there was a piercing sound of broken glass. A blond youth in his early twenties had crashed through a window onto the balcony. There, in full view of the other students, he started scratching himself ape fashion. Everyone laughed, including Graham. "That young man reminds me of my ancestors," Billy quipped. The students whistled and applauded. That was when he added, "Of course, all my ancestors came from

Britain." They cheered even louder. After that, everyone listened attentively. Later Billy said, "I don't think I made many converts. But then, who knows? God does move mysteriously!"

Later, he spoke to a large group of upperclassmen at Cambridge University's School of Divinity. It was obvious their orientation was far more liberal than his, and they had come to heckle. As is his custom, Billy prefaced his remarks with "The Bible tells us . . ." One student was so indignant that he shouted, "Really—you can't expect us to swallow that nonsense! Assuredly, even you are aware that man has progressed far beyond."

He was silenced, but it was very apparent that many of the others shared the accuser's viewpoint when they yelled, "Hear! Hear!"

Billy remained composed. There were a few more interruptions—several students rattled their chairs and issued some bland catcalls. However, most of them decided to listen quietly. Near the end of his talk, the American evangelist said, "I assume we are all Christians. And as Christians we love one another. A minister is not a minister unless he is winning people to Christ. If theological students don't think they can do that, they should quit studying for the ministry."

When he finished, they applauded and cheered for five minutes. This time their "Hear! Hear!" was intended for him.

By the end of the crusade's first week, newspapers reported that people were fighting for tickets. Police estimated that it was not unusual to have crowds of 25,000 or more standing outside the arena. Billy was flattered when he was invited to take tea at Lambeth Palace with the Archbishop of

Canterbury: "I was so jittery that Ruth had to pull me up short. In her practical way she said, 'Any man who has six sons, even if he's an archbishop, has to be an ordinary man.'

"He was far from ordinary," Billy said. "But upon meeting him, he instantly made me feel at ease."

Ruth spent most of her days in London assisting her husband and counseling converts. Those who discovered that she was Mrs. Billy Graham wanted to know the secret of her happy marriage. Repeatedly, she told them, "Bill and I live for each other, and together for God."

On one occasion her participation was not ecclesiastical. It happened near the Hyde Park corner. Ruth was on her way back to the hotel when it started to rain. She hadn't taken her umbrella, so she ran for shelter. Suddenly, a young man appeared at her side.

"You look like somebody badly in need of help," he said. "Why don't we wait out the rain over a cup of tea?"

"No, thank you," she replied. "I'm on my way back to my hotel."

"You must be an American. Even they can take time out for tea. It's jolly good."

"I simply have to get back. But thanks anyway."

"Well, how about tomorrow night?"

"That would be impossible. I have to be at Haringey for the revival meeting."

"Then the next night?"

"Thank you, but it's off to Haringey again."

"I'm afraid to ask, but I suppose it's Haringey the night after?"

"Yes."

"You wouldn't be connected with Billy Graham, would you?"

"His wife," she replied, laughing. "But I do hope you'll come."

"I . . . might," he grunted as he made a rapid departure.

When Billy learned about the attempted pickup, he was elated that he was married to such an attractive woman. "Ruth gets prettier and prettier with each passing year. I keep telling her that. Everybody loves to get compliments."

One of the born-again Christians whom Ruth counseled was British actress Joan Windmill. "The first thought that came into my mind when I saw her," the stage and screen star said, "was how much sooner people like me would have come to Christ if we had met a few attractive Christians like her . . . and at the time I hadn't known that she was Billy Graham's wife.

"She told me that her Bible is always handy. That when she gets a free moment she turns to it. She said that recently she had been faced with a problem and turned to Psalm 37, which says, 'Trust the Lord.' With great sincerity she explained that, 'I believe I live in that Psalm. We must trust Him. We have to know He loves us and has a wonderful plan for our lives if we give Him a chance. Yes, we must trust in the Lord."

More than 2 million people attended the English sessions. Declarations for Christ poured forward from the humble and the mighty. Among the prominent were the First Sea Lord; Sir John Hunt, leader of the expedition that conquered Mt. Everest; and the Admiral of the British Fleet.

One convert who was famous for an entirely different reason was a much-jailed pickpocket. After listening to the American evangelist, he mumbled to the man sitting next to him. "Now I'll have to return your wallet to you; I slipped it out of your jacket pocket a few minutes ago."

Although his conversion didn't last very long—he was shortly apprehended again—Billy claimed that others did. Many asked, "Aren't you afraid that a decision made in a few minutes won't last?"

He had a ready answer: "When I met my wife, I decided in minutes that I wanted to marry her. It was the same way when at sixteen years of age I attended a revival service like this. I walked forward and made a decision. I made a calm, quiet resolve in my heart to live for Him from that moment on. I have lasted. I personally know hundreds of married couples, factory workers, business executives and professional people who have lasted.

"We're not strong enough to hold on to Christ—He holds on to us. There is a doctor back in the States who was on the alcoholic skids until several years ago. His practice was gone and his family had about given up hope for him when he was converted in a campaign. After the decision he did an about-face. His practice is now booming and he has a happy Christian home.

"An acquaintance cornered the doctor recently and said, 'Now tell me the truth, Doc. If you were all alone where there was no possibility of anyone ever finding out, wouldn't you take another drink? Let's be honest with each other.' The doctor thought for a minute before replying. 'Yes, if I were all alone I think I would take another drink.' After a short pause he added, 'But I'm never alone. Christ is always with me.' "

Ruth also had a reply to these skeptics. Indignantly, she said, "People don't crowd around a nursery window and whisper as they gaze at the newborn babies, 'But will they live?' They know that doctors and nurses and mothers and fathers will be trying to make sure they do live.

"Often the reason that some of the 'baby' Christians don't last is that nobody helps them. They are terribly in need of somebody who will teach them how to use stumbling blocks for stepping-stones, somebody who will pick them up and dust them off when they fall. There is a poignant voice in Ecclesiastes 4:10 . . . 'Woe to him that is alone when he falleth.'

"Yes," she continued, "there are those who do not last—as surveys have revealed. But no survey can ever show how the zeal of one Christ-dedicated life touches another and another and goes on and on!"

After the new disciples march down the aisles, churches of their choice are notified. If the minister dallies too long—the Team checks—the name is sent to another church. During the greater London crusade, the Archbishop of Canterbury was making his rounds. In one Church of England he visited, the minister told him that he had received the names of two would-be members from the American Evangelical Team.

"You had better call on those people right off," the Archbishop cautioned. "If you don't, Billy Graham will send their names to a Baptist church."

Now that Billy was an international celebrity, his presence

was eagerly sought. The House of Commons gave a luncheon in his honor. Queen Elizabeth and Prince Philip requested that the Grahams dine at Windsor Castle.

Ruth relished telling an anecdote about the royal meeting: "Bill was so excited that upon entering the palace he heartily shook the hand of the liveried man who opened the door. It was the butler."

A short while later he committed the same *faux pas*. This time he and Ruth were guests of the Duke and Duchess of Hamilton, the Queen's representatives to the Church of Scotland. The evangelist rented formal clothes for the occasion. After being introduced to the other guests, he found himself facing a very distinguished-looking gentleman. Bowing low, Billy said, 'How do you do, your grace? I don't believe we've met.' "

The startled man stepped back. "I am your waiter, sir," he muttered haughtily.

Graham admitted that he was very embarrassed, but later when he told friends about the incident he asked, "After all, wasn't he also created in God's image?"

Near the conclusion of the crusade, Billy, who had been trying to arrange a meeting with Winston Churchill, was summoned to No. 10 Downing Street. They shook hands. Then the aging Prime Minister, holding an unlit cigar, stared silently at his visitor. Suddenly he pointed to three newspapers lying on a table. "Look at them," he said sadly. "They carry headlines about murder, robbery and rape. I'm an old man without any hope for the world. What hope do you have for the future?"

"Mr. Prime Minister, I'm filled with hope," Graham replied

as he withdrew a small Bible from his jacket pocket. "Life can be exciting. This book tells of God's plan for the future—and it's wonderful!"

Again, Churchill was silent. Then he mumbled, "Yes, what you say may be our only hope."

The next time they met, Churchill wasn't so pessimistic. "Billy," he said, "the people certainly believe in you. I don't think Marilyn Monroe or any other Hollywood celebrity, performing in London free-of-charge, could draw bigger crowds than you did!"

Billy was asked to conduct rallies at Hyde Park and Trafalgar Square. The throngs were so overwhelming that on the last day of the crusade it was decided to hold rallies at two mammoth stadiums: Wembley, London's largest outdoor arena (capacity 120,000) and White City (70,000) were selected. They are several miles apart, and Billy managed to shuttle back and forth through tremendous mobs. Ticket demands were so great that large numbers of people camped all night.

The Lord Mayor and members of Parliament were present at Wembley, and the Archbishop of Canterbury gave the benediction. When Graham started to preach, there was a sudden stillness. "You couldn't hear any other sound—no one coughed—no one moved," reported the *News of the World*, a Sunday newspaper that claimed the largest circulation in the western world. "There was no emotional hysteria, no tension . . . only a very deep reverence. Within minutes of his windup, thousands of men and women and teenagers were moving to the track. They were of all ages, of all classes of society. Husbands and wives were hand in hand with their children."

The Archbishop was so touched that he said, "We'll never see such a sight again until we get to heaven." Grady Wilson, one of Billy's chief associates, put his arm around the prelate and hugged him. "Brother Archbishop, you're so right!" he said joyfully.

Most of the English newspapers sharply altered their opinions of the American evangelist before he left their country. William Connor (who signed himself "Cassandra"), a popular columnist for the London *Daily Mirror,* had been among the most vitriolic journalists. He often referred to Billy as the "the dollar-loving blighter from North Carolina."

As the crusade drew to a close, Graham agreed to dine with him in The Baptist's Head, a well-known London pub. After the meeting, Connor wrote: "He came into The Baptist's Head absolutely at home—a teetotaler and abstainer able to make himself completely at ease in the spit and sawdust department, a most difficult thing to do. . . .

"Billy Graham looks ill. He has lost fourteen pounds in this nonstop merciless campaign. But this fact he can carry back to North Carolina with him. It is that in this country, battered and squeezed as no victorious nation has ever been before and disillusioned almost beyond belief, he has been welcomed with an exuberance that almost makes us blush behind our precious Anglo-Saxon reserve.

"I never thought that friendliness had such a sharp cutting edge. I never thought that simplicity could cudgel us sinners so damned hard. We live and learn."

8
THEN,
NEW YORK CITY

FOR YEARS, BILLY'S burning desire was to carry the Gospel to New York City, which he felt to be sorely in need of spiritual revival. Finally, in 1957, his wish was granted. The Protestant Council of the City of New York, representing 1700 churches of thirty different denominations, asked him to come.

"I go in fear and trembling," he told Ruth. "I'm prepared to be crucified by my critics, but I feel I must go."

Dr. Reinhold Niebuhr, the respected liberal theologian, claimed that Billy would invade New York promising a "new life" to his converts, "not through painful religious experiences but merely by signing a decision card."

However, Graham's most hostile belittlers were extreme fundamentalists like Dr. Bob Jones, Sr. (the same man who years earlier had told Billy that he'd be a misfit anywhere), who attacked Billy for "inviting modernists to kidnap him."

Jones was reported to have posted a notice in his school warning students not to hold prayer meetings that "beseeched God to render Billy's New York Crusade a success."

Graham said, "As Ruth had done so many times before, she gave me the strength I needed. She instilled so much confidence in me that when I was handed the anticipated seven-figure budget I wasn't a bit worried. I thought, 'If a big corporation can spend millions of dollars on a campaign to sell a bar of soap, why can't far less than that be spent to tell the message of God's promise of salvation?' "

He formed an executive committee of prominent New Yorkers to help supervise the crusade. Among those selected were Dr. Norman Vincent Peale, the internationally known Protestant minister; Captain Eddie Rickenbacker, World War I flying ace; Ogden Reid, editor of the New York *Herald Tribune;* and Roger Hull, president of Mutual Life of New York. They leased Manhattan's largest indoor arena, Madison Square Garden, for sixteen weeks. When Billy heard about it, some of his doubts returned. Ruth reminded him, "With God, all things are possible."

The Grahams accepted an offer to be the guests of a leading hotel. Norman "Red" Pearson, the bellman who escorted them to their room, recalled, "I showed them in first, then went outside to get their luggage. When I got back, what do I find? The two of them bending down to pray. I can spot phonies right off—those two weren't!

"They didn't even seem bashful that I caught them. Instead, Billy tells me, 'Praying makes me feel good all over. Does it do the same to you?' I answered, 'I'm afraid it's not for me—I lean to winning on the ponies.' He and his wife laughed. She said something about God giving out with sure winners.

"Just about that time it hit me who I'm talking to. But there weren't any airs about them. Billy handed me two tickets for his opening night. 'Bring your wife,' he said.

"I did. All through Billy's sermon I kept nudging her. 'Imagine, he talked directly to me!' It was the same with the gas station I deal with. They gave out free bumper stickers that advertised the crusade. As I took one, I said, 'Yeah, I know Graham personally. He's a good friend of mine.' "

That quality formed the lead paragraph of a story that appeared in the New York *Journal American:* "Billy Graham, the Southern evangelist, has learned a most profound secret: You feel his piercing eyes riveted on you and his heart with you. . . . Instantly you become his friend."

Dorothy Kilgallen, a columnist for the newspaper, prepared an affectionate five-part biography. In one of the installments she referred to Billy and his wife as a "dazzling advertisement for the state of matrimony." Kilgallen said that when she next saw Ruth, she was told, "Bill and I aren't so unique. Every marriage that admits God can become a dazzling advertisement for matrimony."

Ruth also spoke about Kilgallen's reference to Billy's constant jumping to his feet every time a woman entered the room. The reporter, who had visited the Graham's home in Montreat, counted twelve separate occasions in a single hour. "You've made poor Bill so self-conscious," Ruth said, "that to be on the safe side he now stands all the time. To give him some much-needed rest I purposely keep out of his way."

The *Herald Tribune,* which had recently started using

pictures of pretty girls on their front page, decided that Billy's visit was an excellent opportunity to run a large photograph of his attractive wife. A reader wrote, "At long last I have a pinup that I think the Lord approves of."

Another newspaper, the comprehensive *New York Times,* faced a special problem—how to address the evangelist properly. They disliked using diminutives, but felt his formal name: William Franklin Graham, might cause some confusion. After several meetings, the editors settled for "the Rev. Dr. Billy Graham." They also decided to publish the entire forty-five-minute text of his first sermon. This was not an easy task, as Billy was speaking ad-lib. He took his text from Isaiah: "Ah sinful nation, a people laden with iniquity. . . . Your country is desolate, your cities are burned with fire: your land, strangers devour it in your presence. . . . If ye be willing and obedient, ye shall eat the good of the land. . . ."

Then he told the hushed crowd, "We have not come to put on a show or an entertainment. We believe that there are many people here tonight that have hungry hearts—all your life you've been searching for peace and joy, happiness, forgiveness. I want to tell you, before you leave Madison Square Garden this night, you can find everything that you have been searching for, in Christ. . . ."

When Ruth read the sermon in the next day's newspaper, she remarked, "Seeing this in print makes me sad I'm a Christian."

A shocked Billy asked, "Why?"

"It would be so wonderful to make a decision after hearing you," she replied.

"I'm merely God's messenger," he reminded her humbly.

"Bill's humility is truly heartfelt," Ruth said. "Here he was a celebrity in his own right. Yet, he was so thrilled when Ethel Waters, the Negro blues singer, started attending the crusade sessions, and referring to him as, 'my child.' One night he asked me in complete sincerity, 'Do you think Miss Waters would regard me as being too pushy if I asked her for an autographed picture?'"

Midway through his appearance at Madison Square Garden, a reporter from *Look* magazine wanted to write a story about him from the angle of the handsome Hollywood type who became the world's leading evangelist. "Billy promptly refused," recalled an aide. "He told me that he certainly wasn't a handsome Hollywood type."

Sonja Henie, the Norwegian ice skater who later became a leading actress, attended the New York crusade. "Billy could easily have become a famous star," she said. "He is good-looking enough. And it is clear that he has much talent. I once asked him why he hadn't gone to Hollywood and made himself a fortune. 'With your reputation,' I said, 'you could easily demand big, serious roles.'

" 'But I do play a big role,' he answered. 'And one of the most serious ones in the world.' "

The *Herald Tribune* called his preaching "A rich mixture of solemnity and humorous anecdote." One night Billy told his audience about "some Texans who decided to play a practical joke on a fellow Texan. We've been hearing a great deal about how everything in that part of the country is on a grand scale. Well, recently some mighty rich Texas oil men dropped a pack of sedatives in the coffee of a fellow Texan. The victim passed out immediately. They carried him to a newly dug grave and left him there in a fancy, custom-made coffin. The next morning when the hungover man awakened he felt the satin in the casket and wondered where he was. He stood up to find out. That's when he saw all the tombstones. And all of a sudden he exclaimed, 'Hallelujah! It's Resurrection Morning and a Texan is the first up!' "

Quickly, Graham raised a forefinger and asked, "Where will you be on Resurrection Morning? It's coming! Will you be an unredeemed sinner condemned to hell? I want you to listen tonight not only with your ears, but the Bible teaches that your heart also has ears. Listen with your soul tonight. Forget me as the speaker, listen only to the message that God would have you to retain from what is to be said tonight.

"Few people really want to do wrong. But they do it. Few people want to be sinners. But they are. What is wrong? The Bible calls it sin. I know we don't like to admit it. We would like to give it some other terminology; that would be easier on our egos. But during this crusade I am going to use Biblical terminology. I do not intend to beat around the bush and skirt the basic issues of life and death!"

He didn't.

Billy has always had the ability to use simple but firm language. When he is commended for it, he often tells listeners about Dr. Karl Barth: "Some years ago the outstanding Swiss theologian—perhaps the greatest of his generation—was lecturing in the United States. He was asked by a young divinity student what was the supreme single thought that ever crossed his mind. Dr. Barth bowed his head and puffed on his pipe. He didn't speak for several minutes—it was very apparent that he was giving the question a great deal of thought. Then he slowly lifted his shaggy head. The audience were on the edge of their seats prepared for some tremendous statement. 'The greatest ever,' he told them, was: *Jesus loves me, that I know, for the Bible tells me so.*'

"Now that's profound," Billy adds. "But it is also very simple. I think this was the secret of the teachings of Jesus. He talked to people who were illiterate, but they understood him. He used little stories—everyday happenings to illustrate great spiritual truths. He made it so simple that all the people could understand him. I think this is the kind of preaching and teaching we need today in the field of religion."

"Billy follows that example," said Dr. Koji Honda, a leading Japanese evangelist. "Even children understand what he's saying and are not bored by him."

Donna Wannamaker, of White Plains, New York, was thirteen years old when she attended the Garden meeting. "I came with my sitter," she said. "My parents are divorced and my mother hired Mrs. Reiss to take care of me while she worked or went out on a date. I lived most of the time with my mother. Every other weekend and the Christmas and Thanksgiving holidays I spent with my father. I did a lot of shuffling around. But it wasn't so bad. In fact, at the time I thought it a pretty neat arrangement. I remember that I shamefully played one parent against the other. It worked. I'd tell my father about the big doll my mother just gave me and he'd buy me an even bigger one. Or I'd say to my mother, 'Daddy is so nice. He lets me stay up until 10 o'clock!' She'd try to outdo him and wouldn't put me to bed until 10:15. But despite all of that

I felt that something important was lacking. Don't for a minute think that young children aren't aware of that.

"Billy Graham had such an effect on me. It's not fair to dismiss it as some childish notion. It was far removed from that. At the end of the evening, he said, 'Your whole life can be completely changed if you come to Christ! Come now!'

"I did. There were temporary moments when I retreated back to the way I was. But it was only temporary. For the most part, I think I've remained a good Christian."

Other than a few minor incidents, the New York crusade was declared a huge success.

One occurred when a retired mathematics teacher shouted, "Dr. Graham, even my students would realize your counting is faulty! You said, 'Christ came on this earth 2000 years ago.' That's wrong. It was 1957 years ago!"

Billy chuckled at the interference. "Whatever the exact year was, we should be forever thankful that He made His appearance." Then he resumed his sermon. "If church people would start living as Christ taught, we would have a spiritual revival that would move the whole world. We have the power to do it!"

When the evangelist finished speaking, he was besieged by autograph hunters. After signing a great many books, an aide called a halt and whisked him out through a side door.

"I worry about that," Billy said. "Did I hurt someone's feelings? This always nags at me. When I'm out I think that I should have smiled at somebody or perhaps have stopped to offer some help."

He recalled walking along a New York street and seeing a

drunkard lying on the sidewalk. "I passed right on. But I kept thinking how Jesus would have stopped and taken time with that forlorn man. I felt terribly guilty."

So guilty that he backtracked. He found a telephone and arranged to pay $75 for an ambulance that took the man to a Salvation Army shelter. The following day he visited him.

Walter Winchell, the late gossip columnist, learned about the incident. He telephoned the evangelist to get more details. "All Billy would tell me," Winchell said, "was that sometimes we forget that we are all part of God's family."

9
MY HUSBAND IS
BILLY GRAHAM

THE EVANGELIST WAS away from home for weeks and months
at a time. "Neither Ruth nor I enjoyed being separated any
more than other couples who are in love," he said. "After
much prayer, we both felt that we could take no other course.
Being away from her was the most difficult thing I've had to
do. After she'd leave me at the train station or airport, I'd feel
like crying. I just couldn't bear to think of being three or four
weeks without her."

His wife has often been asked if the prolonged absences
made her lonely. "Occasionally," she confessed, "I went to
bed with his tweed jacket for company. But there was little
opportunity for self-pity. Little Grahams were constantly
underfoot. I don't think God ever really called me to be a
missionary. It was like when Bill was young and dreamed of
becoming a big-league ballplayer. We all have a dream. But
it worked out very well because later when he started
traveling around the world, instead of resenting his going, I

got a tremendous vicarious thrill out of what he was doing."

Early in the marriage, Ruth tried to spend a few days at each of her husband's crusades. However, as the family grew, she decided that her first duty was to the children: "If at all possible, a mother's place should be in the home. Children are perceptive. They know if their mother is working for an extra color TV set or because the family cannot do without the money she earns. A mother has to remember that she has the most enviable position in the world. Rearing children is a tremendous responsibility and an enjoyable job. I feel that we mothers are homemakers by divine appointment. We are put here by God to perform a divinely appointed task."

Women's liberation groups might take sharp issue with Ruth's position on the female role. "Marriage is the greatest career a woman can have," she insists. "Her home should be her primary interest. In a Christian marriage, the responsibility falls on the wife's shoulders to adjust to her husband."

To many, this attitude would appear to be extremely far behind the times. "She is extreme in only one area," said Dr. Lois Ferm, a longtime family friend and director of the Billy Graham Oral History Program. "And that is her deep love of God. With all heart and soul she believes that God created woman to be an helpmeet. She is that helpmeet's most sincere defender. Once when Billy asked her what she thought of a sermon he had just delivered, she replied, 'It was fine except for the timing.' He wanted to know what she meant. 'You preached eleven minutes on a wife's duty to her husband and only seven minutes on a husband's duty to his wife.'"

During the 1954 crusade in London, Ruth was browsing through the stacks of secondhand religious tracts in Foyle's, a large bookstore. A distressed-looking clerk darted out from behind the shelves. "Aren't you Mrs. Billy Graham?" he asked. "I desperately need your help!" He poured out his story: a marriage that was breaking up, a wife who was uncertain of her role, unhappy children, and a job that was threatened by his discontent.

Ruth determined that the man was an absentee husband and an absentee father. She urged him to attend the revival services Billy was conducting. As she was about to leave she told him, "You have to be prepared to work for happiness!"

A year later, Ruth, who has a passion for old books, was again shopping at Foyle's. She met the same clerk. This time he was beaming. He had taken her advice and had gone to the revival meeting and there made a declaration for the way of Christ. He was happy to report that his marriage had improved tremendously: "My wife has never been in more cheerful spirits. My children are thriving."

Some years later, the Grahams visited London once again for a series of religious meetings. At one of them a man approached Ruth. She instantly recognized the Foyle's salesman. This time he introduced her to his family, who were all then engaged in "doing God's work."

"Mrs. Graham," his wife said, "you were so right when you told my husband, 'You get out of marriage what you are prepared to put into it.'"

Ruth was pleased that she was credited with providing help. "But," she said, "it was clearly visible when I first talked to him that he and his wife so badly needed to believe in Jesus Christ. They just weren't aware of it. Too often, people aren't."

When someone compliments Ruth, she quickly changes the subject or offers some amusing anecdote. "That clerk in the bookstore was one of the few people in London who didn't have a title," she joked. "Over there, all we met seemed to be lords and ladies. Everybody with some lofty rank—and me with a homemade dress that had zipper trouble!"

Her sense of humor is always evident. When Billy was courting her, he said he would like to meet Dr. and Mrs. Bell. He telephoned for directions from the village. Ruth, who had warned him that the area was filled with hillbillies, pulled down her long, dark hair, blacked out a tooth, took off her shoes and walked down the road barefoot to meet him. She had disguised herself so well that he drove right by.

She enjoys poking gentle fun at people who take themselves too seriously. One dinner guest who insisted on endless bragging about his achievements was served tadpoles swimming in muddy water for the soup course. He was about to hold forth on his favorite subject—himself—when he noticed the strange contents of his bowl. He put down his spoon, gulped several times and remained silent the rest of the evening.

At Thanksgiving some years ago, Ruth felt some members of her family weren't paying proper attention to the significance of the holiday. She substituted shaving cream for whipped cream on the pumpkin pie—after that, everyone was very aware of that special day.

"It's amazing how little she worries about what people think," said a former neighbor. "She believes in trying to do what she knows is right and not wasting time caring what people are saying. Once I attended a school meeting with her. Most of the well-to-do mothers were all for buying fancy

Christmas presents for the teachers. Ruth said it sounded more like a bribe. And she didn't mince words when she expressed her feelings although she said them calmly.

"This refusal to be provoked," the neighbor continued, "seemed to release great spurts of energy. She'd write poetry, build stone walls and kill ever-present rattlesnakes. She'd go around in blue jeans and flat sandals. Once she told me the reason for that was because she could never tell when an emergency would occur. 'So I dress accordingly,' she explained."

When Ruth Graham goes out in public, her picture is completely different. She carefully coiffes her hair, puts on lipstick and dons fashionable clothes. A Hollywood reporter who interviewed her when she attended the Tournament of Roses in Pasadena wrote, "Billy Graham's wife fits perfectly into our neighborhood. She could easily be mistaken for a movie star."

Her husband was proud of the description, but he said, "That newsman is only half right. I agree that Ruth's pretty as an actress. Why, she even gets whistles at Bible colleges. But she possesses far more than just physical beauty. Something many Hollywood stars don't have—a special radiance that comes from the love of God!"

There is admiration for each other's appearance. Ruth once told her mother, "Bill looks now just the way I used to think my ideal man would be. He certainly didn't look like that when I married him. Do you remember what a beanpole he was then? But he's filled out over the years. When he's home, I often find myself looking at him with intense pride and pleasure."

Thirty-eight-year-old Harvey Cutler, a salesman for an

Atlanta, Georgia, mobile home company, claims that this mutual esteem played a large role in returning him to the Lord: "I guess you'd call me a confirmed look-away southerner. We always had a Confederate flag flying in front of our house and a large picture of Robert E. Lee in the living room. My mother tells me that I could sing 'Dixie' long before I learned 'The Farmer in the Dell.' So you see that good manners and courtesy went down along with hog and hominy.

"I was considered a crackerjack salesman. True, everything I said and promised customers wasn't exactly the complete truth, but it did get results. Because of my sales record I won a free trip to Florida for two—all expenses paid. My wife, Edna, and I were on our way back when the Grahams got on the same plane and sat down right in front of us. 'With them here,' I kidded Edna, 'there can't possibly be a crash. God just wouldn't allow something bad to happen to Billy!'

"I eyed the Grahams' every move. He bowed all over the plane when he gave his wife the window seat. She kept on thanking him. Then he made sure she was comfortable. I'm pretty tall and could see them perfectly. He put his arm around her and they kissed. I knew they weren't exactly spring chickens, but they acted that way. I don't mean they did anything raunchy, but it was pretty clear they liked each other a whole lot.

"During the flight they did a great deal of talking. I leaned forward so I could hear them better. They discussed the Bible, money, hunger, people who were not able to read. Even animals. She told him she thought one of their dogs needed tender loving care. He asked her a great many questions, then he'd listen respectfully, nod and say, 'Honey, you're quite right,' or 'Dear, now it's clear to me.'

"When it came time to get off the plane, he waited until she was in front of him. He put his hand on her shoulder as if to keep trouble away. It had been a long while since I saw such consideration and good manners. I was right behind him and shook his hand as we waited for the door to open. Billy introduced me to his wife and I did the same. Mrs. Graham, who looks like a shorter version of her husband, said, 'I see you also had a vacation. It does help to wind down.'

"Edna and I went to church regularly, but it never really made much of an impression. Now it seemed different. We told our pastor about meeting the Grahams. He wanted to know all the details and had me speak to the entire congregation. Edna and I were so moved by the whole thing that we both decided to accept the Lord again.

"It probably sounds like a silly reason and that we did it because of an ego trip. We've talked about it a great deal. I think what really pushed us forward was something Mrs. Graham told Billy. He asked her if she was sorry the vacation was over. 'Not for a moment,' she answered. 'It will be such a joy to return to the serenity of our home.'

"You see, we didn't feel that way—we never had a real home!"

Some visitors would regard the Grahams' household as anything but tranquil. "One of the peculiar things about living in a preacher's family," said Ruth, "is the way strangers expect to see halos. For all our striving to make God the center of our home, life in the Billy Graham household is not a matter of uninterrupted sweetness and light."

She once described it as "Noah's Ark of happy confusion." Billy felt that keeping a large variety of pets provided an excellent opportunity for teaching their children the facts of life. His wife agreed but said wistfully. "Why can't I just tell them and save us a lot of bother and money?"

She has always managed the family's finances. In the early days of their marriage, it presented some problems, as she was frequently overdrawn on her checking account. She recalled, "Whenever I heard that nice Mr. Hickey from the bank say over the phone, 'Ruth, this is Bill Hickey, uh—how are you?' I'd know it's not my health that concerned him. I'd reply, 'Oh, dear, have I done it again?' He was always patient. Eventually I learned to add and subtract."

Josephine Haggerman certainly couldn't be considered a leading exponent of Ruth's theories on the female role. She is married but uses her maiden name. She has a four-year-old son who attends a day care center while his mother serves as a primary school teacher. "Yet," she said recently, "after listening to Ruth Graham on the Phil Donahue television show where she made a guest appearance and reading her book of poetry—I've become impressed by her understanding of our problems.

"We don't live too far away from the Grahams and occasionally I'd see her when I was out shopping. I went to school with her son Franklin. So it was with special interest that I watched her on television. When she was asked if she was a liberated woman, she smiled and said, 'Yes, I am. I'm liberated from having to earn a living so I can devote my time to my family and home.' She told him that before Jesus came along women didn't have a chance. She said that she regards the Bible as the best book ever written on women's liberation as well as child-rearing.

"I was moved by her utter sincerity. I reasoned that any woman who can be such an exceptional wife and mother has to have pretty sound ideas. Especially when she said that love between family members should include a large measure of respect—that deference for each other is a very necessary ingredient. I gathered that the Grahams are very much a mutual admiration society." Then she added, "But on second thought I guess they're more than that—a mutual admiration society for all Christians—that is those they believe are truly Christians."

Billy is frequently asked, "What is a Christian?" He often replies in a Socratic fashion by posing his own query. "Do you think it is a person who is born in a Christian home?" Before the individual can reply, he thunders, "No! I could be born in a garage, but that doesn't make me an automobile! You can be born in a Christian home and have fine Christian parents, but it does not automatically make you a Christian. You cannot inherit Christianity!"

10
OUR DADDY IS
BILLY GRAHAM

JUST AS THE shoemaker's children are proverbially barefoot, it is a cliché that the sons and daughters of evangelists come to grief. And suicide, constant brushes with the authorities, violent marital discord and exceedingly antisocial behavior are certainly more noticeable when the culprit is a minister's child.

One young man, whose revivalist father tirelessly preached salvation to sinners, was accused of theft. Bitterly, he told the police, "Sure, I'm guilty as all hell. But then so are my parents! My mother felt her place was always alongside my old man, who was forever rescuing others—never had a minute left to provide their own kids with a normal home."

The five Graham children are leading happy and productive lives. Virginia and Anne, the two oldest children, were quickly joined by Bunny and Franklin; Ned, the youngest, was born six years later in 1958. Adults now, they are an exceptionally appealing-looking clan, and practice the religious routines of worship that they were taught at home.

"Their well-being is all due to Ruth," Billy acknowledges. "While I was on the go, she remained at their side. When they needed her, she was there. Ruth feels strongly that a mother's job is the most important one in the world, and that no preacher ever gets as close to anyone as a mother does to a child she holds on her lap.

"She often emphasized this viewpoint with a story Dwight Moody, an earlier famed evangelist, used to tell. He was once approached by a mother of six who said she suddenly had the call to preach. 'You certainly have,' Moody agreed fervently. 'And your congregation is waiting—all six of them!' "

Ruth, in turn, credits her husband for the Graham children's equanimity. "Despite Bill's frequent absences," she insists, "he was a far better father than many male parents who are always home for dinner. He made sure that they knew what his values were. Not just by telling them, but by showing them. He taught them how to grow up loving the Lord.

"When they were very young, Bill managed to enter their make-believe world with enthusiasm as great as theirs. Oh, I know it wasn't always easy. But then, Christ never promised that it would be easy."

"Right from the start," observed a neighbor, "it was pretty evident that the Grahams intended to use the Bible for their Dr. Spock. At the time I was pregnant with my first, Gigi [Virginia] Graham was two years old. She was a lovely little girl. So, as a matter of course, I turned to Gigi's mother for child-rearing instruction. I remember Ruth saying to me that Proverbs 22:6 offered the greatest advice she had ever discovered. It certainly worked wonders for her brood":

> *Train up a child in the way he should go: and when he is old, he will not depart from it.*

Virginia

The eldest Graham child is married to Dr. Stephen Tchividjian, a psychologist of Armenian descent. They were wed in an ancient stone church overlooking Lake Geneva in Clarens, Switzerland. She was seventeen, the bridegroom twenty-three. Billy performed the service. He told reporters, "Stephen is one of the most dedicated young Christians I have ever met. He is the only man in the world to whom I'd give my daughter in marriage at her age."

Virginia recalled, "When my sisters and I were growing up, Daddy took us to a remote mountain spot and told us to pray for the boys we would eventually marry. 'You're still quite young,' he said. 'But God has already made the selections.'

"At the time some of us may have thought it silly, but I realize now how fortunate I was to be born in a family that believed so strongly in the power of prayer. My parents prayed and loved me before I ever entered this world. Once, when Stephen and I and our children visited Montreat, Daddy said, 'Remember, the most important thing in rearing a family is each person's relationship to the Lord. All things flow from that."

She describes herself as a Christian, a wife, a daughter, a mother and a friend. Ruth endorses that characterization. "Gigi is grand in all five categories," she says.

The editor of a national magazine once tried to hire the Grahams' eldest child for his cover. "She has all the requirements to be a top professional model," he said. "Pretty, tall and curvy."

"All the credit belongs to my parents," Virginia told a journalist. "The only thing they didn't do enough of when we children were young was to argue in front of us. We never heard a cross word. One result was that when I married and my husband and I had our first argument, it shook me up, because I thought that wasn't supposed to happen. But then as Stephen and I got older, we realized that they had had their arguments, but they kept them from us. In every other area they were excellent examples.

"I was always aware of how much love existed between Mother, Daddy and God," she says. "Stephen and I have tried to pass it on to our children. Once we asked them what they thought marriage was. Our oldest, who was quite young at the time, exclaimed, 'It's when you find somebody you want to keep!' "

Ruth believes that every parent should have one Virginia to raise: "She was a terror one moment and an angel the next. One time she got into some mischief and when I questioned her about it, she replied, 'Mother, you can't blame me. It wasn't my fault. It was the devil! He's the one that got into me and made me do it!' All of a sudden she noticed the expression on my face and said, 'But, Mother, as soon as he saw you coming, he left.' "

When Virginia was pregnant with her second child, Ruth composed a poem in her honor and sent it to her as a Mother's Day gift:

It seems but yesterday
you lay
new in my arms.
Into our lives you brought
sunshine
and laughter
play—
showers, too,
and song.
Headstrong,
heartstrong,
gay,
tender beyond believing,
simple in faith,
clear-eyed,
shy,
eager for life—
you left us
rich in memories,
little wife.
And now today
I hear you say
words wise beyond your years;
I watch you play
with your small son,
tenderest of mothers.
Years slip away—
today
we are mothers
together.

Anne

A member of the Bible study class the second Graham

daughter teaches said, "Not only is Anne lovely-looking and brainy, she is also so sincere in her love of God that it's practically impossible not to be affected by that love."

Anne Morrow Graham Lotz was born in 1948. She is married to Dr. Daniel Lotz, a former star basketball player who became a dentist. Together with their children they live in Raleigh, North Carolina. She was about to enter college when she asked her parents' permission to be allowed to drop out of school in order to marry Lotz, eleven years her senior.

"She was very young," said Ruth, "but Bill and I realized how much they loved each other. We agreed that it would be foolish to make them wait. Besides, some of the most interesting people I know never went to college. They made up for it by reading. And some of the dullest I have met graduated cum laude."

"Our middle daughter was usually the kindest of children," Billy recalled. "However, one afternoon her mother heard her shouting orders, followed by moans. It was coming from the kitchen. Ruth rushed in to find five-year-old Anne slapping her two-and-a-half-year-old sister in the face. After stopping the one-sided brawl, she demanded to know what was going on. Anne replied sweetly, 'It's all right, Mother. I'm just teaching her the Bible—how to turn the other cheek.' "

Anne looks and sounds like her father. She is tall and long-legged; she possesses many of his mannerisms, including his speaking ability. There is frequently an extensive waiting list for her Bible class. She takes her religion seriously and has the skill to make it interesting. It was due to her urging that Billy conducted a crusade in Raleigh, her adopted home-town.

She values privacy and doesn't often discuss her family. "Daddy is sharing everything else with the world," she said. "This part of his life is ours alone. People may think it's because we're not a close family, since we're awfully spread out, mileage-wise. But we're close in spirit and we absolutely adore our parents. They set the tone of our lives by the way they lived theirs. Their dependence on God was obvious— Mother's light would be on late at night and early in the morning as she studied her Bible and prayed. And Daddy, even though the world acclaimed him as a great man, and so many sought him for advice, would still get on his knees and humbly ask the Lord for guidance.

"Through all of this we learned that seeking God was not a sign of weakness but a sign of strength and knowledge of ourselves—we are not complete persons until we allow Him to take control; then we become that for which we were created. This wasn't taught to us in a dry pious manner, but with an abundance of happiness."

A local minister, writing in his church bulletin, once castigated Billy for harboring reactionary ideas. Anne quickly dashed off a letter to a Raleigh newspaper, stoutly defending her father. "The naiveté of this type of criticism amuses me," she wrote. "This critic assumes that because Dr. Graham is a friend and spiritual counselor to kings, queens, presidents and leaders, that he sanctions their various policies and practices of government."

Anne does have one wryly amusing story about her father. Some years ago she drove him to the Asheville, North Carolina, airport. It was extremely crowded and as usual dozens of people came up to greet him. When the time came to board the plane, Anne turned to hug him. That was when the preoccupied evangelist reached for his daughter's hand, shook it firmly and murmured, "It was so nice to meet you."

Bunny (Ruth)

"It is not surprising that my first memory is of my family kneeling in the living room for prayers," recalled the Graham's middle child, who was born in 1950. "Prayers were held during or after breakfast and again at supper. To be honest, there were times we groaned when we heard the familiar call, 'Prayers.' But today each one of us children has family prayers in our own homes.

"Many people pray as if God were a big aspirin pill. They pray only when they are hurt. But Mother and Daddy taught us to pray about everything. Daddy has said, 'The Lord is not so busy with great affairs of the universe that He cannot bother about these little lives of ours.'

"In a world where there is so much insecurity and no absolutes and so much confusion, there is no greater assurance than to know that we can always be in touch with the King of Kings, Lord of Lords, and Ruler of the Universe."

It's likely that a listener would get an unflattering impression of any person who mouthed such lofty phrases. Joan Ratner Heilman, who interviewed her for *Good Housekeeping* magazine, said, "She isn't the dowdy and oppressively pious stereotype one might expect in a preacher's daughter. She's a strikingly pretty woman. Tall and slender, with long blonde hair, porcelain skin and deep blue eyes. She wears lipstick, blue eye shadow and swinging clothes."

Ruth endorsed the description. She objected, however, to one of the words: "The clothes are not *swinging*," she said. "They are *stylish!*"

Like her two older sisters, Bunny is greatly in demand to teach Bible classes. The minister of a church she attended said, "Billy's daughter has a special gift of communicating God's word. I've listened to her and found myself thrilled at her skill in making the Bible come so alive."

Bunny's husband, Ted Dienhart, is an advertising executive for a firm that lists the Billy Graham Evangelistic Association as one of its largest clients. "People call at all hours begging to get in my wife's Bible class," he said.

"From the moment Bunny arrived," Ruth recalled, "she was good. I feel that God realizes that exhausted parents occasionally need one like her. She'd play happily in her crib for hours. Rarely cried. She was the sort of a child who did things without being nagged. She always had a wonderful disposition and would make us laugh with her sense of the ridiculous."

One day Bunny's mother discovered that the youngster had a great many coins in the tiny purse she had been given at Easter. "This was very strange," Ruth said, "since she only received an allowance of twenty-five cents a week. I questioned her about it. She cheerfully admitted, 'Nice people give me money to stand still while they snap my picture. If I smile a lot they give me a nickel extra. So I always smile.' "

There were times when the laughter gave way to tears. "Children have very real problems," Billy said. "They worry deeply about them. To them it's just as important and far reaching as an adult facing a major crisis. Unfortunately, I wasn't home often enough to offer my full support. But when I was there I tried so very hard to be a good listener. Over the years I've discovered how necessary it is to listen respectfully when a child is despondent. And not to dismiss their complaints as nonsense."

Once the evangelist returned briefly from Washington, D.C., where he'd met with the President of the United States. He was exhausted. He wanted to shave and change his clothes before leaving for an important meeting. Bunny intercepted him with a serious worry. She threw her arms around him as she poured out her woes.

"We talked for a long time," Billy said "I was late for my meeting, but I'm glad I knew where the priorities were."

Bunny well recalls that occasion. "Busy as Daddy was, he spent time, he loved me, he prayed with me, he cried with me. That will always be a very special memory, that Daddy would take time from his busy and tiring schedule to share his daughter's burden."

Franklin

William Franklin Graham III, son and namesake of the world-renowned evangelist, said, "My father accepted God because he chose to do so. I had to do the same—my way."

The first three Graham children were girls. Billy and Ruth hoped the next one would be a boy. When he was about to arrive, the evangelist was conducting a crusade in Texas. Informed that his wife was in the early stages of labor, he rushed back to Montreat in time to escort her to the hospital. He was with Ruth until she was wheeled into the delivery room. A short while later, a nurse told him that his wife and new son were doing fine.

"I was so excited," Billy recalled, "I jumped high in the air and let out a happy yell that you could hear all over the hospital."

Ruth insisted on naming the infant William Franklin Graham. Billy reluctantly agreed, with the provision that the boy would be called Franklin. In Boone, North Carolina, where he and his wife, the former Jane Austin Cunningham, and their three sons make their home, he is known as "Frank Graham, the fun-loving doer of good."

He is considered one of the town's leading citizens. He heads a nonprofit missionary organization, World Medical Mission, which among its many overseas pursuits recruits physicians for Third World countries. Recently, he was ordained into the ministry, which started rumors, that he had been chosen to succeed his sixty-five-year-old parent. "God gave my father a special talent," he said. "One that he can't pass on by his own choice."

Billy also discounted the reports about his son's being groomed to take over: "Franklin has repeatedly told the press that he would never follow in my footsteps. He's very much his own man and makes his own decisions. Besides, I have no plans for retirement."

Nevertheless, he and his wife were overjoyed when Franklin was ordained. Billy embraced his son and pronounced the occasion "a culmination of my life."

Ruth, merrily, but with visible relief, jested, "In case anyone worries about a son being away from God, stop fretting. Nobody is hopeless."

Although Franklin made his first decision for Christ at the age of eight, he had strayed far afield in the course of growing up.

At the time Ruth observed, "I think Franklin is rebelling against being a preacher's son. Especially that the preacher happens to be a famous one."

Adverse publicity arrived only too soon. A popular columnist wrote: "The handsome son of evangelist Billy Graham was out nightclubbing until the wee hours with the pretty daughter of songstress Lena Horne!" At the time Franklin was only nine years old. Although the columnist printed a retraction, it was an accurate forecast of what was to come.

"We prayed," Billy recalled, "that until Franklin realized he was wrong and came back to spiritual living, our love would hold him up."

When Franklin's third child was born, Ruth wrote a poem about her son's early days:

> God,
> look who my Daddy is!
> He is the one
> who wore his guardian angel out
> (he thought it fun).
> First, it was bikes:
> he tore around those hills
> like something wild,
> breaking his bones
> in one of many spills;
> next, it was cars:
> how fast he drove (though well)
> only patrolmen
> and his guardian angel knew;

the first complained,
the second never tells . . .
Not long ago
You touched him,
and he turned,
Oh, Lord, what grace!
(And how quizzical the look
upon his angel's face:
a sort of skidding-to-a-stop
to change his pace.)

And know, he just had me:
which only shows
who needs a little angel of his own
to keep him on his toes.
Oh, humorous vengeance!
Recompense—with fun!
I'll keep *him* busy, Lord.
Well done! Well done!

Ned

Billy was present during the birth of his younger son. The
evangelist was very moved by the experience. "How can
anyone doubt God's presence after witnessing such a miracle?" he asked. "The infant's first cries are the language of
beauty, order, perfection and intelligence—God's work!"

The new baby was named Nelson Edman for his maternal
grandfather, Dr. Nelson Bell, and for Dr. Raymond Edman,
president of Wheaton College, where the infant's parents had
met.

"From his earliest days Ned showed a passion for the out-of-doors," said his mother. The angelic-looking, blond, blue-eyed youngster was always wandering in the woods. "I knew where to find him. He'd be out collecting rocks or leaves or wild flowers. It seemed that he had a different hobby each week, all somehow connected to nature."

The older Graham children had attended local schools, but Billy and Ruth decided to send Ned to a very austere English boarding school. "It was so strict," the boy's father said, "they made the unruly students strip down and sit in ice cold water for an hour whenever they broke a rule."

Ned was brought back to the States after a year and sent to a private school in Stonybrook, New York. An excellent swimmer, Ned won several cups in school competitions. His coach felt that with more experience he could make the Olympic team, but Ned quickly dismissed the idea. "I don't plan on staying in the water for eight hours at a stretch!" he said.

Ned took a year's sabbatical to think things through. He got a job as a salesman in a sporting goods store that specialized in rock-climbing equipment. "Ned is an expert in that field," said his mother. "Also in tennis and karate." She believes that his temporary academic recess helped him sort things out. "His relationship with the Lord is solid," she feels. "If anything, it's increasing. He's a very devoted young man." Presently, Ned is working on his bachelors degree. He and his wife, Carol, a nurse, live on the west coast. They met when she treated him for a leg injury.

"God was very wise when he made that selection," said the proud father-in-law. "I'm certain that Carol will bring as much happiness to Ned as Ruth has given me."

In his sermons, Billy frequently refers to his children. "They often help me make a point," he says. During a crusade in Houston, he told his audience, "One day I was walking along the road with my son Ned, who was then five years of age. We stepped on an anthill. We killed a lot of ants and wounded many others. 'Wouldn't it be wonderful,' I said to him, 'if we could go down there and help those ants rebuild their house and bury their dead, take care of their wounded?'

"He looked up at me. Then he said, 'But, Daddy, we are too big. We can't get down there and help those ants.'

"I thought for a moment. 'Wouldn't it be wonderful if we could become an ant and live in an ant world?' And that is exactly what God did. God Almighty decided to become a man and that is who Jesus Christ was. My young son seemed to understand what I was saying."

Several years before Ned was born, the Grahams decided they needed living quarters that provided more privacy, for Billy's fame was rapidly growing. Streams of the curious drove up to their very accessible home and gawked. They peeked in the kitchen window to see what Ruth was cooking, gathered flowers for souvenirs, took photographs of the children.

"It was terribly annoying," Ruth recalled, "but I felt we had learned to cope with the lack of privacy. It got to be a family joke. I'd claim that if the sightseeing cars drove quickly by, they were probably from the Episcopal center. If they slowed down, they were Presbyterians. Then there were the ones that actually stopped, got out of their cars and wandered all over. They were the Baptists. Bill used to kid me that I was prejudiced against the Baptists. But that's the way they were. They were so friendly. Sometimes, too friendly!"

The Grahams wished to continue living in the Montreat area and looked at many remote land parcels. They particularly liked a 200-acre plot located at the edge of the Blue Ridge Mountains. A narrow, winding, single-lane road, practicable only by Jeep, led to it. That suited them very well. The evangelist said, "The land was very cheap—$13 an acre. However, the owner wanted to sell the entire tract. We decided, reluctantly, that it was too costly."

One day when Billy was on the west coast a very determined woman, armed with a large box camera, knocked on the Grahams' back door. When she learned that several of the children were taking afternoon naps, she demanded that they be awakened so she could get a group snapshot.

"That did it," Ruth said. "I felt something had to be done immediately. I borrowed money from the bank and bought that terrific piece of Blue Ridge land we had both liked so much."

With help from friends they built a house with a superb mountain view. A stream was dammed to make a swimming pond for the children. "I thought our wish for privacy might hurt them," Billy said. "Granted, there weren't many playmates around, but they did have each other and that seemed to be enough. They were always doing something. Sometimes too much!"

The Graham children were physically punished for willful misbehavior, for the evangelist and his wife believe that

sparing the rod spoils the child. They feel that parental
responsibility involves giving the youngster what he or she
needs—and frequently that need means physical discipline.
"Coddling children," Billy said, "avoiding correction, is one
of the primary causes of delinquency. The parent who takes
the time and the trouble to discipline his child loves him far
more than does the namby-pamby parent who sows the seeds
of delinquency in overlooking and tolerating antisocial
action. Children actually welcome being disciplined."

Once, when the Graham children were still quite young,
the usually mild-mannered Anne told her mother, "You aren't
such a sweet person. You spank people."

"Mother has to do that," Virginia quickly said. "If she
doesn't spank us when we are bad, God will punish her."

Three-year-old Franklin had other ideas. Billy disciplined
him for striking one of his sisters. "Now, if you had a little
boy who was mean to his sister, what would you do?"

Franklin, always able to think rapidly, replied, "I would
not spank him!"

Father and son talked about children hitting each other.
Then Billy suggested that he and Franklin pray over the
offense. They knelt down. The youngster's prayer was: "Dear
God, please forgive me for hitting my sister. And forgive her
for all the times she has hit me."

While most of the discipline problems were easily solved,
Ruth was always afraid that one of them would surely find its
way to the newspapers. During a crusade in Florida, she
brought her two older daughters for a brief visit. While she
was resting in a Miami hotel room, the girls were amusing
themselves on the roof garden. Suddenly Billy burst in.

"Looks like we have a lawsuit on our hands!" he shouted. "The girls have been throwing rocks and the desk clerk just told me they hit a woman on the head!"

Aware that a reporter who had written several unfavorable crusade stories was in the lobby, Ruth rushed out to find her daughters. They had disappeared from the roof garden. After a great deal of searching, she discovered them locked in a tiny broom closet. Despite her pleas, they refused to leave their hiding place. In desperation, Ruth found an electric cord, which she shoved under the door. After several thrusts, the girls decided that their mother was really enraged and reluctantly came out.

Ruth was convinced that the journalist would uncover all the details and print a disapproving story. She could imagine the headline: EVANGELIST'S WIFE BEATS DAUGHTERS WITH ELECTRIC CORD!

Although the children occasionally sported slightly red backsides, they vigorously endorse their parents' discipline theory. "It worked because Mother and Daddy were just and firm," said Bunny. "Rules were carefully spelled out. If they were broken, punishment followed swiftly. Usually a shoe tree applied to the bottom by Mother. She did most of the disciplining. But neither ever punished in anger.

"I can remember distinctly that Daddy only spanked me three times. All for very good reasons: once for lying, once for kicking Franklin in the head, and once for telling Mother that I hated her. But when it was all over, we'd pray together and ask for guidance, and Daddy would always gather me in his arms and tell me that he loved me. Mother would do the same."

Ruth drew up a list, prompted from Proverbs, entitled "A mother must . . ."

1. Walk with God.
2. Put happiness in the home before neatness.
3. Not be the victim of her own disposition.
4. Make her tongue the law of kindness.
5. In discipline, be firm but patient.
6. Teach that right means behaving as well as believing.
7. Not only teach, but live.
8. Not only speak, but listen.
9. Realize that to lead her child to Christ is her greatest privilege.

People who know the evangelist's wife regard her as a very practical person. "She tells it as it is," said a storekeeper who has done business with the family for years. "I remember the time she gave one of my customers quite a tongue lashing. This other lady came in with a dog on a leash. He was very frisky and knocked over several unopened cartons. That's when his owner beat him real hard. It got Mrs. Graham very angry."

Ruth loves dogs and has owned and appreciated many of them. Recently she said, "Dog trainers seem to know more about child-rearing than some parents. In many households the dogs are better trained than the children." She says quite seriously that every parent should get hold of a good book on dog obedience. "Follow the rules," she advises. "They are very simple."

1. Keep commands at a minimum. One word to a command and always the same word.
2. Be consistent.

3. Be persistent. Never give a command without seeing it obeyed.
4. Offer praise when the command is carried out.

"It's not true that Bill and I had no major problems with our children," she admits. "Each crisis has taught us so much of God and also compassion and understanding for each other. Granted there were headaches and heartaches, but they were far overshadowed by all the joys our children brought. Who can forget Franklin's first night when he decided to camp out on our front porch? In the morning I asked the youngster if he hadn't been worried that the polecat might come around.

" 'No, ma'am,' he replied.

'Why not?' I asked.

'I had my gun with me.'

'Honey, that wasn't a real gun!'

'But, Mom, the polecat didn't know that!' "

Her husband shares her thoughts on children. Several years ago he told a crusade audience that he wouldn't want his daughters to meet Elvis Presley for fear of contamination. Hearing of this, Presley was deeply hurt. "I admire Billy a whole lot," the singer said. "I wouldn't dream of putting a finger on anyone from his family."

To which Graham replied, "That's good, since I regard every child as part of my family."

"Ruthie feels exactly the way her husband does," said Ethel Waters. The late black songstress and actress frequently performed at Billy's revival meetings. "I learned what love really is from that precious child," she told a *New York Times* reporter. "I'll never forget the night when I was with the crusade in London. At the time I had a bad foot and was trying to leave before the huge crowds started pouring out. That's when I ran into her on the stairway. She was holding on to a teenaged girl who was so drugged, her eyes were rolling—she was really on a trip. Somehow the girl had gotten into the meeting and had almost passed out.

"There was delicate little Ruthie, half-carrying, half-dragging this girl who was twice her size. She was a dirty, hippie type—smelled like she hadn't taken a bath in months. But that didn't seem to bother Ruthie. She was soothing this girl. Embracing her. Showing her the love of God. Showing her that someone cared."

Ruth spends a great deal of time counseling troubled young people. Once when she talked to a group of inmates at a reformatory, a pretty fourteen-year-old brunette, who had been committed for habitual shoplifting, told her, "More than anything else I'd like to be part of a happy home."

"What's your definition of a place like that?" Ruth wanted to know.

"It's where the mother and father like each other and also their kids," the delinquent girl replied. "And are not afraid to show it." Then she added wistfully, "But I guess that's expecting too much—homes like that happen only in the movies." The other girls nodded in agreement.

"I don't want to blame parents for all of society's ills," Billy said. "But shouldn't every child be entitled to a happy home? In today's world too many of our youngsters are 'orphaned' by the total disintegration of the family. Millions of mothers and fathers have abdicated their proper parental roles."

The Grahams are both of the opinion that a truly satisfying

home has to be based on disciplined and obedient children. "I've often said that the reason our own children turned out well," Billy observed, "was because their mother managed them with a Bible in one hand and a rod in the other. Of course, punishment must be meted out carefully and compassionately in the spirit of love. However, I've discovered that a great many parents are confused when it comes to discipline. They are afraid physical punishment will bring on hate. As a matter of fact, the reverse is true. A child that's permitted to defy convention constantly, often grows up to be a discontented adult, bringing grief to himself, his mother and father.

"Not long ago a woman complained to me about her unruly son. 'I can't understand his rebellious behavior,' she confided. 'All I ever do is give him a pat on the back.' I quickly replied, 'Madam, perhaps that's where the trouble lies. Why don't you try applying your pat lower down?'

"Young children," Billy added, "will invariably talk, walk, think, respond and act like their parents. Give them a target to shoot at. Give them a goal to work toward. Give them a pattern which they can see clearly and you give them something that gold and silver cannot buy."

11
CHRISTMAS
AT MONTREAT

Christmas love is close at hand,
About to embrace all the land.
The holy days are here we know,
When comes forth Billy's TV show.

Several years ago this bit of doggerel appeared in a weekly
New Hampshire newspaper, heralding the start of the holiday
season. Whenever his frenzied schedule allows, the evangelist tries to share Christmas with television viewers. On the
evening of December 24, millions of people around the world
ardently watch Billy and Ruth, the Graham children and their
spouses, grandchildren and friends, who are all on camera
sitting in front of the large, stone fireplace in the living room
of the evangelist's home. Billy often wears a red sweater;
Ruth, a green dress. "For us it's the most thrilling time of the
year," Graham said. With a grandchild perched on his lap, he
reads from the Bible the story of the advent and birth of

Jesus. The reading is followed by prayers and the singing of carols and hymns.

"Billy has a special gift of making Christmas meaningful," observed country singer Johnny Cash, a frequent visitor to their home. "He makes you feel you can almost touch the miracle."

Soon after the program is aired, many ministers report sharp increases in born-again Christians who attribute their renewed conviction and dedication to the Billy Graham show. Here are three case histories:

"I guess for people like me," said Pete Horton, a very fat, very bald and very bowlegged construction worker, "that program officially starts Christmas. This may sound like I'm some kind of unbeliever, which I'm definitely not. But it's like Billy's the baseball umpire who waves his hand and yells, 'Play ball!'

"As a matter of fact, isn't life sort of a ball game? There are winners and losers. Me, I was always on the losing end. It started from the time I was born. I never knew who my parents were. They probably weren't married—leastway, not to each other. Until I was sixteen, I lived in an orphan asylum. Foster homes weren't yet popular in my town. Oh, I'm not going to complain that everything was terrible. That's not true. Just most things!

"Anyway, when it came time to leave the orphanage, they got me a job as maintenance boy in a factory that made paintbrushes. For a while it was okay, but then the whole plant moved to another state. I was out of a job. After a lot of searching I managed to get work in a printshop sweeping and cleaning—things that I had done before. But they had to shut down from lack of business. It went on like that. Nothing lasted.

"I got so disgusted that I joined up with the Army. They made me a cook. Why, I'll never know. Maybe they figured that was the best thing for a bandy-legged GI. My buddies used to say, 'Pete's scrambled eggs taste like poured cement!' Despite that, when I was discharged, I managed to become a fast-order cook—for a single week. But when they started getting complaints about my cooking, I was given the gate. It seemed that no one in his right mind wanted me.

"Then a fellow I knew in the Army told me about a civil service opening for a park attendant. At the time I was living in Boston. I applied and was hired. I was tickled pink. Here was a steady lifetime job that even carried a pension.

"Rita, that's my wife, worked in the park department office as a file clerk. I met her there. I discovered that we had a lot in common—she had also grown up in an orphanage. We started going around steady, then got married. It was good having a regular home and having somebody that cared if you lived or died. The only real trouble we faced was when Rita had a miscarriage. But right after she became pregnant again—the doctor felt it was too soon. Anyway, this time she carried it through and we had a son. He was some kid—weighed almost ten pounds right off. Rita said he was my spitting image. We named him after me.

"Things looked better than ever. There was talk of me becoming a foreman. Then it happened. Two weeks after I got my promotion, young Petie dropped dead in his sleep. We were told it was from a rheumatic heart condition. A doctor once said that Petie's heartbeat was a little off, but claimed we shouldn't worry—that it wasn't serious. He made it sound like it was really nothing.

"Petie's death changed everything. Rita and me started fighting all the time. She blamed me. That I couldn't wait to demand sex right after her miscarriage. It became a regular hang up with her. I tried to tell her that the doctor had assured me that it had nothing to do with it. But that didn't help. Sometimes she'd get me so mad that I'd call her every name in the book and belt her. Rita didn't exactly take it lying down. She'd scratch and kick me. I still have bruises. It got to be such a regular habit that the only thing left was to call it quits—which we did.

"I thumbed my way all over the country—been to forty-five of the fifty states. To earn enough money I'd find small, part-time jobs like parking cars or washing dishes. It was in Eugene, Oregon, that I saw Billy Graham's Christmas Show. Looking at his healthy grandchildren didn't exactly make me happy, but somehow his message got through to me: *that I had another chance!*

"At the orphanage they used to make us go to church. I guarantee that no one listened to what the preacher was saying—least of all me. I never went much for religion and I hadn't looked at a Bible in years. Now, it seemed to matter. Tears started streaming down my cheeks as I thought about how I had messed up my life. I counted the number of commandments I had broken. Billy was saying that at times like this families should be together.

"Wouldn't you know it? That was exactly when the television set broke down. I shook it real hard. Nothing happened.

So I shook it even harder. This time it went back on just as he was saying that to feel alive you had to reach out to God. That with Him in your corner you would wipe out the past. That God loves you and will forgive you.

"For over a month I thought about what Billy Graham had lectured about, but kept putting off making a decision. I guess I was too stubborn to go forward and admit that I desperately needed God's help. But no matter how hard I tried I couldn't put it out of my mind. Over and over I kept thinking about what Graham had said. Finally, I took the plunge and walked into a small Baptist church in Albuquerque, New Mexico. You may find this hard to swallow, but I swear that when I came out I felt different—it was as if a 500-pound weight had suddenly been lifted.

"I hitchhiked back to Boston, where Rita was still living. She wasn't at all happy to see me. The honest truth, she was downright unhappy that I was there. She told me to get lost—that she never wanted to see any part of me again. I remember one time she said, 'Why don't you join the French Foreign Legion? But on second thought, they wouldn't even have you. Peter Horton, you stink out loud!'

"If this had happened earlier, I'm sure I would have blown up and given her a few slaps. This time I didn't take her flat-out. Sure, I was hurt, but I kept coming back. Finally she realized that I was a changed man—that the bad things had left me. We've been back together for five years. Have two healthy and happy children. And, best of all, a healthy and happy marriage. All thanks to Billy Graham and his Christmas Eve Show. I wrote and told him about what he done for one American family."

Everett McCauley's life was also radically altered by Billy's television program. However, his story is very different from the previous one. McCauley is in his late forties. He has often been told that he resembles Cary Grant. The comparison delights him, but he quickly dispells any notion that he's a movie type.

"I prefer the legitimate stage," he said loftily. "What's more, I'm the vice-president and comptroller of a small insurance company. And there's probably nothing more prosaic than that.

"It's the only company I ever worked for; came here immediately following my college graduation. I was earning $48 a week when Elizabeth and I were married. We didn't have much money, but it always was a most satisfactory union. I don't think that during the sixteen years we were man and wife we ever had a serious quarrel.

"There weren't any children. Not that we didn't want any; we tried for years. Medical authorities convinced us that it was impossible. Elizabeth was infertile because of an ovarian tumor. It wouldn't respond to any treatment. We discussed adoption. However, I fear it was only talk. Instead, we got increased pleasure out of each other's company. Selfish pleasure.

"We traveled extensively. Twice a year we'd get to New York to see hit plays. Whenever I had to go out-of-town on business, she'd come along. We spent an inordinate amount of time together. I was pleased when the working day ended so that I could be with her.

"Well, it was too good to last. Shortly after our sixteenth wedding anniversary she had a mastectomy. There was a malignant tumor in her breast. Two months later she died.

"I'm not overstating when I say I became deranged. After her death I didn't go to the office for weeks. Just sat in the house and stared into space. When I finally dragged myself into the office, I just sat there and did some more staring. My associates suggested a long holiday—perhaps a trip around the world. At first I was annoyed at the recommendation. But when our firm's president repeated the suggestion, I took a round-the-world cruise.

"It failed completely. In every exotic port the ship docked, I'd think how Elizabeth would have reacted. It got so bad that I actually started engaging her in conversation. Once, a fairly attractive divorcée invited me to go sightseeing with her. 'Are you husband-shopping?' I asked belligerently. 'I've got a wife!'

"I was glad when the voyage ended. I came to the conclusion that I'd led a good and happy life, but the major part of it was over. The time had come to resign myself to that fact. Nothing could be done to bring Elizabeth back.

"Now everything revolved around the company. Insurance all day long. I would get to the office early and stay late. When I'd get home, I'd turn on the television set and sit there for hours. I'd drift off to sleep in the midst of the late show and wake up, still dressed, to the early-birds' program.

"On Christmas Eve it seemed that all the programs revolved around the holiday. I found myself watching Billy Graham and his self-satisfied-looking family. I rotated the dial, but kept coming back to the Grahams. In spite of my displeasure, I was intrigued. It was so apparent they were a happy group. I noticed the decorated tree in the corner of his living room and it brought back memories of the times Elizabeth and I decorated ours, laughing and throwing on the tinsel. I remembered that I still had all the ornaments stacked away. They hadn't been opened in a long while. This made me quite disturbed. I kept seeing the ornaments glittering through newspaper wrappings.

"The more I watched the show, the more restless I became. But it wasn't a hopeless kind of upset—I find it difficult to describe the feeling. I suppose it was like a swimmer who is about to go down for the third time who suddenly realizes there are things he can do to save himself.

"I didn't rush out to find Jesus Christ. Although Elizabeth and I couldn't be called regular church attenders, we still thought of ourselves as proper Christians. We had never renounced the church. I had been christened soon after my birth. I felt I hadn't strayed. That I was still a Christian. But the Graham Christmas TV Show did something for me—it made me realize that I no longer wanted to be alone. That Elizabeth wouldn't think me evil if I found someone else to share my life. Three years ago I took a new wife. It, too, has been a good marriage."

Paul Atwood's Yuletide transformation was more subtle, but equally as meaningful. Atwood is the forty-three-year-old manager of a supermarket in a large middle-class suburb of Philadelphia. He is proud of serving as a commander in the Naval Reserve. He looks trim in his blue uniform, although his wife recently had to let out the waistband of his trousers two inches.

"It was my daughter, Barbara, who begged us to watch the

show. She had seen it the previous year and thought we should look at it. Kids these days seem to be real interested in religion. So to please her, we did. My wife, Catherine, sat on the couch. Naturally, I sat on the chair the family calls 'Pop's Super Special.' It's a tattered but really comfortable Morris chair that leans all the way back. Barbara and my other daughters, Laura and Nancy, sat on the rug.

"When I took over the supermarket we were at the bottom in volume of business. There are seven food markets in our town—we ranked seventh. Now we are in third place, and, believe me, we're not going to stop there. I make a fairly good salary, but Catherine decided to go back to work after Nancy entered junior high. My wife's a dietician. She got a job in a nearby hospital. I didn't exactly like the idea of her returning to work, but I didn't argue. The money was useful. And besides, Catherine is pretty strong-willed.

"Not that much of what she said affected me. And vice-versa. We went mostly our separate ways. I don't mean to imply that we had one of those modern-style open marriages. I'm sure another man never entered her mind. And I certainly didn't think that way. Except if you count that checkout clerk that kept giving me the eye. We had coffee together a few times, but that's all.

"I can't say that because of Catherine's job the house was sloppy or that the meals came out of cans or that the girls were not cared for adequately. Things seemed to fall into place, but despite that, they didn't seem just right. That Christmas, Billy Graham showed us what was missing. A relationship with God.

"We've become a family. We're really interested in all the

other members. Rod, the butcher in my store, said to me a couple of months ago, 'Paul, I don't know what it is, but you've become more alive.'

"He was so right. I have. I guess you might call me a living, breathing Billy Graham Christmas miracle!"

A cameraman's helper who once worked on the show recalled, "Billy happened by while I was checking some of the equipment. He asked me if I thought he was coming across properly. I told him that I wasn't the best person to ask since I considered myself a dyed-in-the-wool, irrevocable atheist.

"My remark seemed to intrigue him rather than anger him. Respectfully, he wanted to know more about my antireligious sentiments. That's when I said that people who claim there are no atheists in foxholes are off their rocker. I pointed to myself as one of the exceptions. 'When I was in Nam,' I told him, 'and the shells flying all around, I'd just close my eyes and think of a juicy steak smothered in onions. It always worked. I don't think they served juicy steaks in Bethelem.'

"Graham smiled and said, 'That makes me think of something that occurred a few years ago when most of the family visited. On Christmas morning we have breakfast before going to the living room to open the presents. Ruth always serves oyster stew—it's a Bell family tradition. I fear we two are the only ones who like it. As soon as the breakfast meal was over, I thought we should have a prayer. It was longer than I intended. Prayer once started is not within human limits. My grandchildren became impatient. When it was finished, they immediately started running for the living room. My daughter Anne called a halt. She asked them to walk very slowly because she had a movie camera and wanted to take pictures. That's when my oldest grandchild muttered, 'I'm sure Bethlehem was never as miserable as this!'

"As Billy headed back to his seat, he turned toward me and called out, 'Perhaps not juicy steaks, but something far better for the soul!' I suppose a good evangelist has to be quick on his feet. He sure is."

Once, in the midst of a sermon Graham was delivering in Sydney, Australia, a group of teenagers attempted to disrupt the service by tossing a smoke bomb. The auditorium was soon engulfed in fumes. To avoid confusion, Billy quickly said, "There goes the old devil doing his dirty work. But this book will soon clear the air." Vigorously he waved his Bible back and forth.

As the audience cheered, he continued, "It reminds me of the time some other mischief-makers, dressed all in red and armed with pitchforks, charged screaming into a small church back home. They looked and sounded so frightening that everybody rushed for the exit. That is everybody but one sweet old lady who was sitting in a front pew. The ringleader approached her and said, 'Don't think this red outfit makes me Santa Claus! I'm the devil! Aren't you scared of me?'

" 'I know full well who you are,' she replied. 'No, I'm not one bit afraid. After all, I've been on your side for years!' "

At the conclusion of Billy's sermon, hundreds of converts marched down the aisles—including one of the smoke-bomb throwers.

12
ALL THE
PRESIDENTS' MEN

ACTOR-PHILOSOPHER Will Rogers was known for his genial ridicule of governments and political systems. On pork-barreling, he said, "Being a friend of a President of the United States not only puts a feather in your cap, but miraculously helps you feather your nest."

Over the years, seven American presidents have regarded the evangelist from North Carolina as a special friend. Dwight D. Eisenhower was one of them. "It is very clear," he said, "that Will Rogers wasn't talking about someone like Billy Graham when he made that statement. In all the times it was my good fortune to have Billy visit the White House, he never once asked me for a single, solitary thing for himself. To my wife and myself he gave a great deal."

However, Graham's initial encounter with a Chief Executive was an unfortunate experience. A congressman from Massachusetts had arranged a meeting between Billy and Harry Truman. Graham was dressed in a white linen suit, hand-painted tie and spotless white buck shoes. He said he was dressed that way because in summer months Truman wore similar clothes and he wanted to fit right in.

"I was plenty scared," he told a reporter from the *Washington Star*. "Here, I was the son of a simple dairy farmer, face to face with an American president. I tried to reassure myself that he was a former haberdasher, but that fact didn't help much. Everything in the Oval Office looked so majestic!"

Truman quickly announced that the contents of the meeting was strictly off the record. Then he said that he too was a God-fearing Baptist but had qualms about mixing religion with government. He added that he had to be extra cautious because the press was after him, especially "that damn Drew Pearson."

Billy asked if they might have a prayer together. "I suppose there can't be any harm in that," Truman said. Whereupon the evangelist bowed his head and prayed that God would bless the President and give him of His wisdom in dealing with all the difficulties in the country and the world.

Although Graham left by a side door, he was immediately accosted by reporters and photographers, who demanded that he give them all the details. When they learned he had prayed with the President, he was asked to kneel down and repeat the prayer. Obligingly, Billy fell to his knees on the White House lawn while the photographers snapped away. Truman was outraged when he saw the story in evening newspapers. "I never want to see that s.o.b. again!" he angrily told members of his staff. "And you better not invite him to this house or you'll never see me again!"

As soon as Graham got back to Montreat he told Ruth all

about the Truman catastrophe. "I discovered long ago," he said, "how important it is to let your mate know the bad as well as the good. I learned that confiding helps the marriage considerably. Keeps it honest."

The Truman debacle was the only defeat an American president ever handed the evangelist. All succeeding Chief Executives went out of their way to inform the public that Billy Graham was not only their friend, but a close friend. Eisenhower frequently told audiences, "I always keep the Bible that Billy gave me close to my bedside. Mamie says that I won't be without it because he was the one who gave it to me. She's right. I can't think of another person who has a closer ear to the Lord than Billy."

Eisenhower once wrote Graham a letter telling him how he felt: ". . . not only my congratulations on what you are doing, but my hope that you will continue to press and fight for the old-fashioned virtues of integrity, decency and straight-forwardness in public life. I thank the Almighty that you are ready to give full time and energy to this purpose."

The General and the evangelist first met in 1952 at the SHAPE base of operations located near Paris. During a two-hour conversation, Eisenhower repeatedly questioned Billy about his religious philosophy. After getting answers, the future President said sadly, "Those are the same values my mother and father held. I'm afraid being in the Army has made me forget some of them."

Immediately after his nomination, Eisenhower sent for Graham. When the evangelist arrived at Ike's headquarters in Chicago's Blackstone Hotel, Eisenhower wanted to know if Billy had any special suggestions that should be included in the campaign. "I'm not partisan," Graham replied. "As a matter of fact, I'm a Democrat. But I do believe that the country is badly in need of a spiritual revival." He urged the candidate to include this message in his speeches.

Eisenhower did so. Soon after being declared the victor, he again asked Billy for advice. This time the President-elect said that he planned on using a biblical phrase in his inaugural address. Graham suggested several. He also helped Ike decide on a church to join. The five-star military officer confided that during his long years in the Army he had never thought about which Protestant denomination was his.

When Billy asked him which one he'd like to be affiliated with, he replied, "My wife is a Presbyterian. I suppose I would like to be the same."

"There are two Presbyterian churches in Washington I would highly recommend," Billy said. "One is the National Presbyterian and the other is the New York Avenue Presbyterian." The new President eventually joined the former.

During Eisenhower's eight years in the White House, and upon his retirement to Gettysburg, Pennsylvania, Billy was frequently invited to call on him. After one of the visits, the irritated General told an inquisitive reporter, "Billy Graham is my friend. And a friend is supposed to visit! Period!"

The evangelist was one of the last persons to speak to Eisenhower as he lay dying in the Walter Reed Hospital. They discussed heaven and prayed together. The General wanted to know if his sins would be forgiven and if Billy thought he was going to heaven. When the evangelist finished providing answers, the former President said, "Thank you. I'm ready."

On the day of the funeral, Mamie Eisenhower invited Graham to her house. She later told a journalist, "My husband would have wanted me to do exactly that. He so regarded Dr. Graham on such a lofty plane."

John Kennedy, Eisenhower's successor, had been warned by his father to be very leary of the evangelist. "You have to be nice to Billy because of all the adulation part of the public gives him," he cautioned. "But be careful! He's another one of those Protestant preachers who desperately tried to keep Catholics out of the White House."

The newly elected President discovered that his father wasn't completely accurate. Although Graham had been involved in the Roman Catholic controversy, he had played a minor role. In the summer and fall of the campaign, when the religious issue was being hotly discussed, Billy was prudently out of the country.

He returned to the United States in time to hear leading Protestant clergymen predict that the Pope would be one of the President-elect's first visitors. They were astonished when Billy accepted a Palm Beach golf invitation from JFK. Kennedy was intrigued by a story he'd heard about a golf game the evangelist had played at St. Andrews, Scotland. He told Lyndon Johnson about it.

"It seems," Kennedy said, "that Billy hit his ball into a trap called Hell's Bunker. It's fifteen feet below the surface and all sand. Instead of taking penalty strokes and slipping back, he got a ladder and climbed down into the bunker. He desperately tried to hit the ball back to the green, but he kept sifting the sand. Finally, on his fifteenth try, he succeeded. As he

147

came up, he said proudly, 'I couldn't let something called hell defeat me. Now, could I?' "

Kennedy grinned and added, "I figure I have to meet someone with such fierce determination." The meeting had to be canceled because of the birth of the new President's son. It was rescheduled.

"I was impressed by his charm," the evangelist said. "He revealed a restless, probing interest in theology and must have asked me more than a hundred questions about my opinions and attitudes, including the second coming of Jesus Christ and the future triumph of the Kingdom of God. From that day on we became friends."

Shortly after John Kennedy's assassination, Billy told a southern audience that the slain President and he had agreed on many important lessons. Among them were the desperate need for racial harmony and religious tolerance, the dire necessity that the world learn to live in peace, and the brevity of life. "His premature death was a terrible thing. But sometimes we must have a terrible shock to rouse us out of our spiritual neglect and apathy."

Graham recalled that he used the White House as a hotel when Lyndon Johnson, Kennedy's Vice-President, moved in. "He was always trying to keep me there—wouldn't let me leave."

The new President, who described himself as a "deeply religious Texan," was the great-grandson of an evangelist who had brought frontier hero Sam Houston to Christ. Johnson was very proud of that conversion and frequently boasted about it. He felt that with Billy's help he could give the

American people "shots of godliness they so badly needed." Presidential appointments are usually scheduled for fifteen minutes. Billy's first meeting with the new Chief Executive lasted five hours.

A story the President enjoyed repeating concerned a joint press conference that he held with Graham shortly before the 1964 national election. Billy told reporters that although he enjoyed Johnson's company, he was going to remain politically neutral. This didn't stop the President from proclaiming that the evangelist was the greatest religious leader alive. Graham felt that he had to return the compliment and said that Johnson was the greatest political leader of the twentieth century.

A few days later, one of Billy's daughters announced that she was going to support Johnson's Republican opponent, Barry Goldwater. The President read about the endorsement and immediately telephoned Graham. "You may be an outstanding religious leader," he said, "but you can't even influence your own family in politics."

Several weeks went by and Johnson's younger daughter declared that she intended to become Roman Catholic. This time it was Billy who telephoned. "You may be a great political leader," he told the President, "but you don't seem to have much influence over your family's religious life."

Johnson was delighted by the phone call and assigned an airplane to transport Billy to his Texas ranch. There the evangelist was asked to conduct services, causing the President to remark proudly, "I personally have the best preacher in all of Christendom."

Billy and Ruth were guests of the Johnsons on the last

weekend the President and Lady Bird occupied the executive mansion. The President, who had a premonition of death, secured a promise from the evangelist that he would preach at his funeral. (Billy kept that vow.) He also handed Billy a note that read: "Your prayers and your friendship helped to sustain a president in hours of need. No one will ever know how much you helped lighten my load or how much warmth you brought into our house."

Many people would rate Billy's friendship with Richard Nixon as his major presidential association. Graham said, "I've known him for a long time—for many years. He was a close friend. I feel that I didn't misjudge him, but I misjudged what he would do under pressure. I think there came a point when he cracked under all those pressures and was no longer the Nixon I had known and admired."

Billy met the future President when Nixon was a member of the U.S. Senate. The two men became good friends, played golf and exchanged family visits. They became even more intimate when Nixon was chosen as Vice-President. In 1960, the controversial political figure decided to seek the top office and asked the evangelist to be his running mate. Graham said he was flattered but quickly replied, "God has called me to preach the Gospel, and I consider that the highest calling in the world."

Later, Nixon claimed that the offer was made in "pure jest." However, a close aide said, "He wasn't exactly kidding. He figured with Billy Graham's name on the ticket, he'd be a certain shoo-in."

Nixon lost that election but was victorious eight years later when he defeated Hubert Humphrey. Shortly after the final vote was counted, the President-elect proposed that Billy join his cabinet or become an ambassador to a major country. Again, Graham refused. "I respect him for his answer," Nixon told reporters. "But I have to say that the country is the loser. Billy is truly one of the giants of our time."

The press was aware of the President's awe of the evangelist. One columnist referred to Graham as "Nixon's man behind the scenes." Billy contends that his influence was highly exaggerated. "I actually saw less of him than I had of Eisenhower or Johnson."

This may be accurate, but as Gerald Strober, one of Billy's chroniclers, pointed out, "There is little doubt that Graham's friendship with Nixon deepened during the Californian's first term in office. Graham was reported as saying, 'It is wonderful for a clergyman to have a friendship with a president.' "

Strober, a reputable, skilled journalist who has spent considerable hours with the evangelist, said, "The two men met and talked with each other often. During one thirty-seven-week period in the spring of 1969, Graham flew with Nixon in Air Force One to a dedication ceremony, took part in a meeting of the Richard Nixon Foundation, stayed at the western White House in San Clemente and was one of the two clergymen invited by Nixon to attend a dinner honoring the astronauts. He also golfed with the President."

During the early days of Watergate, Billy defended Nixon. He told one television interviewer, "His moral and ethical principles wouldn't allow him to do anything illegal like that. I've known him for a long time and he has a very strong sense of integrity."

As more and more evidence began to pile up, the evangelist started expressing doubts. He kept repeating, "There must be two men there!" Finally, in May of 1974, there was no further question about Nixon's complicity. Graham released a statement that appeared on the front page of the *New York Times:* "What comes through in these tapes is not the man I've known. . . . Our repudiation of wrongdoing and our condemnation of evil must be tempered by compassion for the wrongdoers. Many a stone is being cast by persons whose own lives could not bear like scrutiny. Therefore we dare not be self-righteous."

Ruth said, "Watergate was the hardest thing that Bill ever went through personally."

Graham knew Gerald Ford when he was a member of the House of Representatives. "I always thought a lot of him," said the man who succeeded Nixon. "But my admiration grew when I moved into the White House. Not only does Billy love his country, but all the people in it."

The evangelist was very pleased when Ford granted a full pardon to his predecessor. "It was a wise decision. Watergate has already done irrevocable harm. Keeping it alive might well have split the nation into two warring camps."

In the spring of 1975, Graham was to give the benediction at a Bicentennial celebration that featured an address by Ford. Ruth was in the audience and became enraged when a twenty-seven-year-old demonstrator waved a sign that blocked out her view of the President. She grabbed the poster which read: EAT THE RICH. DON'T TREAD ON ME.

When Ford was told of her action, he said, "Mrs. Graham,

like her husband, reveres the office of the President of the United States." He was amused when he learned that she had later handed the young man a Bible.

"Instead of carrying that ridiculous sign," she had said, "I suggest you spend your time reading these marked passages."

Jimmy Carter, who replaced Ford, met Billy during a Georgia crusade. He had personally invited the evangelist. "I know from firsthand experience the great beneficial impact of your crusades for Christ," Carter wrote. "It would be a meaningful experience for the people of Georgia if you came here to share with us your commitment to our Lord."

The evangelist agreed to preach. He tried to get a prominent Georgian to serve as chairman. More than a dozen VIPs were approached. They all refused because Billy insisted that the crusade be fully integrated. Carter had to do the presiding.

When he became President, he promptly invited Graham to the White House. Billy went, but ever since the Nixon experience he had been extremely careful not to be accused of doling out secular advice. He was determined to limit his discussions to religious matters only. He and Carter had long talks about the strong need of Americans to seek God. "I value Billy's counseling on Jesus Christ," the southern President said. "I'm grateful that I have been privileged to know him."

Billy was equally impressed. He told a reporter from the *Washington Post,* "I think President Carter's bringing a new spirit to the country. God has a place of honor in the White House."

Ronald Reagan, the current occupant of the executive mansion, is also an old friend. He, too, admits to having a very high opinion of the evangelist: "And why not? I had decisive evidence of his tremendous effectiveness when I was governor of California."

At the time, Reagan discovered that one of his aides was having severe marital problems. After listening to the troubled husband, he advised him to read Billy's book *The Secret of Happiness*. "It may sound like too simple a solution," Reagan said. "But with my own eyes, I saw how well it worked. That man and his wife were surely headed for the divorce courts. Now they are enjoying an excellent marriage. I give a great deal of credit to Billy's book."

Though mixing closely with assorted American presidents, Billy has retained some of his early roots. Marshall Frady, author of one of the most comprehensive Graham biographies, best described this phenomenon: "From his boyhood on his father's farm, there still seems a quality about him, like a lingering ambiance from all those years of milking twenty cows every day, of fresh cream and butter and custard, a certain pasteurized dairy-like mildness."

Harry Truman, several months before his death, said he was quickly aware of that farm background: "You may think you're taking the country out of the boy, but you can never fool another farmer—he knows right off. The minute I laid eyes on Billy I could detect where he grew up. He'll carry that hay and straw smell with him to the grave. The ministry needs people who come from the soil."

Not everyone can readily spot Billy's rural origins. Ruth

once attended a luncheon where her husband was the guest of honor. When he finished his speech, the woman sitting next to her whispered, "I'm very surprised to learn that he milked cows when he was a boy." Then she gushed, "He's so eloquent and handsome. To think he was raised on a farm! With that background isn't it a shame that he isn't in politics?"

"Maybe the Lord thought politics had its share and decided to give the ministry a break," Ruth replied.

Recently, John Robinson, a reporter for the Raleigh *News and Observer*, asked Billy to describe himself. "I'm a little bit lazy," the evangelist replied. "Totally dependent upon God because I know I have so little to offer myself. A little shy, which people don't see probably, but I am. I have a hard time just going up to somebody and introducing myself and speaking to them."

13
TO RUSSIA
WITH LOVE

MANY OF GRAHAM'S staunchest supporters felt that his influence as an evangelist ended when he returned from his 1982 trip to Moscow. Even the White House condemned the mission. He was accused of ignoring the plight of Soviet Christians and Jews and telling the Russians that religious freedom existed in their country.

What he actually said was that he himself did not observe any lack of religious freedom in the Soviet Union. His remarks were poorly reported and quickly misrepresented. Typical was a headline that appeared in a Virginia newspaper: BILLY HOODWINKED BY COMMUNISTS!

The usually sympathetic *Time* magazine questioned the wisdom of his visit: "Graham seemed oblivious to the precarious role of religion in a country that endorses scientific atheism and outlaws public evangelism."

Conservative columnist George Will called Billy "America's most embarrassing export."

The New York *Daily News*, a long and loud advocate of Billy's crusades, reported, "Graham displayed an extraordinary combination of innocence and ignorance."

Yet, three months later the evangelist's crusade in New England drew overflow crowds. Charles Woodring, a divinity student, attended several of the revival sessions. "Although," he said, "I go to a school that is considered liberal, I certainly don't regard myself as a fellow traveler. Quite the contrary, my classmates know how deeply I'm opposed to anything Red. They claim that I'm so paranoid on the subject that I'm forever seeing radicals under the bed—that I won't even order a cherry soda because of the color.

"However, after hearing Dr. Graham speak, I genuinely believe that he went expressly to spread the love of Jesus Christ to people behind the iron curtain. I think he succeeded despite what all the newspapers printed. It's ridiculous to think for one minute that he was hoodwinked by the Communists. He's much too smart for that. I'm sure the reason for his actions was that he wanted to be invited back to preach a full-scale Crusade for Christ throughout Mother Russia. It seems to be working out exactly the way he planned. Almost immediately after his pilgrimage to the Soviet Union he was asked to make religious trips to East Germany and Czechoslovakia, which he did.

"I only hope that someday I'll be one-tenth as good a servant of God as he is."

At a press conference in New York City, Billy defended the remarks he made in Russia. "If there had been any restrictions on what I wanted to say, I would not have gone," he told reporters. "I would not, of course, pretend in the least to be an expert on the Soviet Union after only five and one-half days in Moscow. I received many impressions that I will, I am sure, be reflecting upon for some time to come. However, my primary goal in going was to preach the Gospel, as I have done all over the world for so many years. I had more opportunities than I ever expected to accomplish this goal. . . .

"Before going I prayed a great deal about it and felt that God had led me. Upon my return I feel even more certain that I was doing His will. It may be some time before the full results of my visit can be evaluated, but even the short-term results are gratifying. . . . After all, the more contact we have, the better."

There is little doubt that over the years some of Graham's views have altered sharply. In 1964 he wrote, "Either Communism or Christianity must die, because it is actually a battle between Christ and anti-Christ." However, in 1982, not only did he deliver an hour-long sermon to a thousand Russians in Moscow's only Baptist church, but he met with several high-ranking members of the Central Committee of the Communist Party.

This ability to reshape his thoughts has attracted many diverse people. Among them was twenty-three-year-old Jonathan Ferris. He, like Charles Woodring, is a divinity student. But unlike Woodring, he considers himself to be "somewhat unorthodox theologically." He explained, "Whereas Charlie is a dyed-in-the-wool fundamentalist who takes every word and comma and period literally, I must confess that I have other interpretations. And listening to Billy Graham hasn't convinced me otherwise. But I will admit that I'm moved by his candidness in owning up to a shift in his social thinking. Hearing him speak made me aware of one very important fact—a person grows—including Christian clergymen.

"I didn't start out to become a minister. If you had asked me when I was a tiny child what I intended to be, I'd immediately reply, 'A doctor.' But when the medical schools I applied to hung out no admission signs, I soon forgot that wish. Instead, I joined the Peace Corps. At the time I was really down on Billy. He had called the Peace Corps a materialistic outfit and said that it couldn't possibly succeed because it didn't have God at its center. I understand he later retracted his statement, but when he said it, he sure got a lot of people irritated.

"You can see that I always had this desire to help. Many's the time I've been called a professional do-gooder. It was in the Virgin Islands, where I was assigned, that I got the idea for the ministry. There was a local Roman Catholic priest who was the most dedicated person I'd ever met. Although I wasn't of his faith, we had long talks. It was he who convinced me that I could perform no greater service. I didn't change my religion, but I figured that becoming a Protestant clergyman would also give me the opportunity to benefit mankind. You may think me silly, but I still feel that way. That is if man doesn't blow himself up before I get ordained.

"Shortly before Billy flew to Moscow, he spoke at Harvard. He talked about many things, including the arms race and the importance of an international meeting that would lead to the destruction of all nuclear weapons. He told us that he intended to spend the rest of his life not only preaching the

Gospel, but working for peace among nations.

"I remember him saying, 'As I searched the Scriptures, my responsibility dawned upon me, and I began to speak out on the subject of peace.' Then he told us that he was still learning. 'The more I learn,' he said, 'the less dogmatic I become.'

"This reached me. I go along with Dr. Harvey Cox, a theology professor at Harvard who is considered one of the outstanding religious thinkers in our country. He said, 'It should give all of us courage that a man in his sixties can grow this way.' "

When the Reverend Jim Jones persuaded 919 of his disciples to drink cyanide-spiked Kool Aid, many people confused the mass suicide with Christianity. Billy was quite concerned. In a widely quoted Op Ed article that was printed in the *New York Times*, the evangelist said, "We have witnessed a false messiah who used the cloak of religion to cover a confused mind filled with a mixture of pseudo-religion, political ambitions, sensual lust, financial dishonesty, and apparently even murder. None of this has anything to do with true faith in God.

". . . as long as man's heart remains unchanged, this type of tragedy will continue to occur—whether in the cold-blooded murders that plague every American city, or the frightening terrorism that stalks so much of the world, or through the wholesale deception of false messiahs like Jim Jones."

Soon after the message appeared, the evangelist received thousands of approving letters. Typical was one from an elderly woman in Arizona who wrote, "Billy, I have to confess that I was pretty confused by those deaths. I kept wondering how a Christian could commit such atrocities. But like always, you made me think twice and then set my mind at ease."

The Reverend Leighton Ford, who is married to Graham's sister Jean, said, "The reason Billy has remained so popular is because he has never stopped growing and closed himself off from new ideas." Ford, who is also a well-known evangelist, adds, "He has maintained the simplicity of his basic message and he has developed greatly in terms of his practical wisdom."

Billy gives a great deal of the credit to Ruth. He has repeatedly stated that one of the functions of a good wife is to aid her husband in maturing. "Ruth's done exactly that," he said. "She has always helped me to think clearly."

An interview the evangelist recently had with journalists Wes Michaelson and Jim Wallis of *Sojourners* magazine, a liberal religious monthly, best reveals that maturity:

Sojourner: How would you describe changes in your thinking on the nuclear arms question, and what factors would you cite as important in prompting those changes?

Graham: It has only been recently that I have given as much attention to this subject as it deserves. I suppose there have been a number of reasons why I have come to be concerned about it. For one thing, during my travels in recent years I have spoken to a number of leaders in many countries. Almost to a person they have been concerned and pessimistic about the nuclear arms race. Second, I think also that I have been helped by other Christians who have been sensitive to this issue. I guess I would have to admit that the older I get the more aware I am of the kind of world my generation has helped shape, and the more concerned I am about doing what I can to give the next generation at least some hope for peace. I ask myself, "What kind of world are my grandchildren going to face?"

Third, I have gone back to the Bible to restudy what it says about the responsibilities we have as peacemakers. I have seen that we must seek the good of the whole human race, and not just the good of any one nation or race.

There have been times in the past when I have, I suppose, confused the kingdom of God with the American way of life. Now, I am grateful for the heritage of our country, and I am thankful for many of its institutions and ideals, in spite of its many faults. But the kingdom of God is not the same as America, and our nation is subject to the judgment of God as much as any other nation.

I have become concerned to build bridges of understanding among nations and want to do whatever I can to help this. We live in a different world than we did a hundred years ago, or even a generation ago. We cannot afford to neglect our duties as global citizens. Like it or not, the world is a very small place, and what one nation does affects all others. That is especially true concerning nuclear weapons. . . . I know one thing—the ultimate hope of the world is the coming of the Prince of Peace—when war shall be no more. Even so, come, Lord Jesus.

Billy has said, "If the Gospel is not more powerful than any ism, I ought to quit preaching."

Some people feel he should. A postcard addressed to the evangelist bore an imperious, one-line scrawl: *"Dear Pope Billy, get lost!"*

Ruth resents anyone speaking unkindly about her husband. "She is not at all defensive about herself," said a family friend. "You can say anything about her you want and she won't take it personally. But when it comes to Billy, it's a totally different story."

Ruth was enraged when all the criticism arose over his trip to Russia. She had to be restrained from offering caustic rebuttals to detractors. One vociferous fault-finder was told about an archeologist she once knew whose hobby was mending broken china and pottery. "He'd spend hours gluing cracked pieces together," she said. "That man reminded me of something God does all the time—carefully and lovingly takes broken pieces of our lives and puts them back together." Then she stared at the person who had the effrontery to attack her Bill. "And that is why my husband went to the Soviet Union," she said indignantly. "To tell the Communists that God will do it for them."

However, she feels quite free to do the dissenting herself. "Both Bill and I speak up for what we think is right," she says. "I fear something is very wrong with a marriage when one of the partners is always in fear of expressing his or her thoughts."

Fraye Gaillard, an editorial writer and columnist for the Charlotte *Observer*, has interviewed both of the Grahams. "In some areas," he said, "she is more conservative than her husband. She offers her thoughts with characteristic bluntness, challenging without apology the flow of his thoughts. They seem to be accustomed to this give-and-take. Their disagreements seem devoid of either coddle or sulk, and he gently hurls the challenge back in her direction.

" 'I'm for capital punishment,' she announces with a tone of finality. 'I think it is a deterrent. I know in countries where they have it, I feel safer walking down the streets.' "

" 'Darling,' Billy replies, 'there are countries where they have executions in which I don't feel safe at all.' "

He has avoided taking a public stand on capital punishment. "I have to be very careful what I say about a great many things," he explained. "My main focus is in the Gospel. But I'm greatly troubled over capital punishment. True, we live in a time of horrible and hideous crime. Is capital punishment the answer? The system has always been one-sided. Most people on death row are poor people who couldn't afford good lawyers. A disproportionate number of them are black. An execution makes it so final."

The evangelist has said repeatedly that when he finds some important issue troubling him, he discusses it with his wife. "That's the way marriage should be. Ruth's often my bell-wether. We lie in bed close together and have long conversations. Those are some of the finest moments."

Ruth likes being Mrs. William Franklin Graham. "In addition to being honored to be Bill's wife, I so enjoy being married to him," she said. Ruth feels that it's within a wife's jurisdiction to poke good-natured fun at her mate. She teases Billy about the time they were vacationing in the south of France. "I looked up the beach," she recalled, "and there was this tall, skinny man wearing red boxer shorts. These were about as common on French beaches as a wedding dress. He had on laced-up Hush Puppies, yellow socks, a baby-blue windbreaker, immense sunglasses and a denim hat pulled down over his ears.

"I thought, 'That's about the weirdest-looking man I've ever seen.' But as he got closer, I moaned, 'Oh, my goodness, he's mine!' "

When she feels that his vanity needs deflating, she delicately yanks him back. "Oh, Bill," she said after he proudly told her about the public embrace he got from the President of

Mexico. "Don't feel too flattered. After all, I saw on television where he did the same thing to Castro."

"There are no airs about her," said a friend. "Some years ago, just before Christmas, she came down with a bad case of the flu. Billy had to take over some of the household chores. Dishwashing included. He wasn't very adept at it—broke several plates. His solution was to give his wife a large, white Christmas present—a shiny new electric dishwasher.

"That was when Ruth told me, 'I always wanted one. What some wives will do to maneuver their husband!'

"How can you avoid loving that woman?"

14
SEX AND
MARRIAGE

RECENTLY, A PROFESSOR of psychology at the University of Southern California queried his students about how they rated the sex lives of practicing Christians. Two classifications were offered: "Dull" and "Lively." A decided majority of those interviewed felt the first category gave an accurate description. Typical replies were:

"Sex is unimportant to those people."

"They rarely discuss it."

"When they do have sex, it's not very satisfactory."

"They feel it's sinful to enjoy sex—only dirty old men do."

Billy sharply disagrees: "Sexual pleasures exist lifelong in a good marriage. However, Christians do feel that sex is sacred, not an instrument of self-indulgence to satisfy your appetite like a fast-food hamburger."

His sermons frequently deal with the subject. Sex, he has said, is the act by which all life on this earth has been created. It should be the most wonderful, the most meaningful, the most satisfying of human experiences. However, it has been made low and cheap and filthy. Too often there is the sly, secret, embarrassed, let's-pretend-it-doesn't-exist attitude. Used rightly, it is a servant of love, to be used as a sensual expression of true unity between husband and wife.

He told one audience, "A man prominent in public life planned the seduction of a beautiful young woman. When she rejected him, he raped her. The wife of a government figure tried to seduce her husband's young associate. When he refused to succumb to her wiles, she charged him with attempted rape, causing his imprisonment.

"Are both of these incidents taken from today's newspapers? No! Though they have a very modern ring, they are taken from the Bible. A book that has never gone out of date, the Bible could properly be called the world's most reliable textbook on sex. No book deals more forthrightly with the subject. As history, it records without distortion the sexual aberrations of its times. As biography, it refuses to gloss over the sins of its heroes, but details them with straightforward explicitness. As philosophy, it sets forth the changeless standards of God. . . .

"Nowhere does the Bible suggest that the battle between the flesh and the spirit is easy. Neither does it suggest that to be tempted is sin. God does not hold you responsible for seeing something which might engender impure thoughts. He holds you responsible for the second look.

"The Bible teaches by precept and example that there are spiritual resources we can use to overcome our illicit urges. . . . For all those caught in a web of sexual confusion and guilt, that there is still the Divine Word. The fact that immorality is rampant throughout the nation doesn't make it right; the fact that some clergymen may condone it doesn't make it right.

"When sex occurs outside wedlock," the evangelist warns, "it only contributes to unhappiness. The adulterer or adultress may boast, 'I cheat on my mate all the time and I don't have any hangups.' Perhaps not yet, but one day soon I guarantee it will take its toll. Misused sex becomes a terrible tyrant!"

Graham has repeatedly pointed out that satisfying sex doesn't just happen. "You have to work at it," he says. "You have to want to make it satisfying. You have to be willing to communicate with your wife or husband. Your mate will never know what pleases you unless you do communicate. I'm not offering you a mess of lofty platitudes. Christian psychiatrists, psychologists, sociologists, marriage counselors, back up what I'm saying. They have all discovered that sexual freedom outside marriage leads to chaos."

Even before turning to God at age sixteen, Billy held that view. His parents told him that the sexual act should be postponed until after the wedding. He is glad they did and happy that he listened. "I shall be eternally grateful. Some of the other fellows in town may have thought me a square. But they were really the squares. All around me I see the misery caused by the wanton use of free sex."

Shortly after Graham became a full-time evangelist, an elderly revivalist told him, "Billy, you better be constantly on your guard. You're young and virile and women are attracted to evangelists—I know."

Many women have tried to place Graham in a compromising position, and he is very careful to leave his door open or to have an associate present whenever he talks to someone of the opposite sex. These precautions are occasionally insufficient. One brazen divorcée attempted to remove her clothes as she loudly announced that she would "gladly sacrifice all privacy for the privilege of serving the evangelist." He fled before she reached her slip.

In the course of a visit to East Berlin, a newspaper reported that a drunken Billy was making the rounds of nightclubs with a blonde draped on each arm. When the revivalist was shown the story, he said, "That poor reporter sure goofed. The night I was supposed to have been whooping it up happened to be the one I was rolling in agony with a kidney stone in the Frankfurt army hospital."

Ruth is not deceived by any of these false plots. "A successful marriage has to be built on mutual trust," she said, "and I know fully that Bill's values coincide with mine."

15
TEN COMMANDMENTS FOR A HAPPY MARRIAGE

EACH YEAR Billy Graham receives thousands of letters from husbands and wives seeking help for love and marriage problems. The writers complain that romance has fled the home, that controversy and dissent occur daily. They are fearful that their marital unions are sentenced to death.

The evangelist replies that if you really want to save your marriage, you can. He points out that despite the alarming divorce statistics, many good marriages do exist. He asks why some work marvelously while others seem to be nothing short of a battleground.

He believes the reasons are not as obscure as some authorities assume and that no dispute exists that cannot be resolved. Billy recalls that when he and Ruth were about to celebrate their thirty-fifth wedding anniversary, a friend wanted to know if the evangelist had ever seriously considered divorce. "No," Graham replied truthfully. "It never even entered my mind."

The next question asked was, "What's your secret?"

Billy said that God has given us certain guidelines for marriage, and when they are neglected, the likelihood of marital difficulty is greatly increased. For years he and Ruth have followed what may be called *The Grahams' Ten Commandments for a Happy Marriage*.

1. *Put God in your marriage*. I mention this first because I am convinced that this is the most important key for a solid marital union. It must have a solid rock upon which to build—it cannot be half and half. If you want certain discord in your home, have deep-seated religious differences. There must be a spiritual understanding.

2. *Learn the art of mutual acceptance*. Respecting each other without constantly wishing things were different is crucial. That doesn't mean a husband or wife simply relaxes and casually decides it is unimportant to change. If the couple honestly wants to improve their marriage, they will seek to overcome irritants. Frustration, disappointment and sorrow are an inevitable part of life. Happiness is hoped for but not promised. It must be merited.

3. *Accept your individual responsibilities*. Not only should the mates accept each other, but they should accept the responsibilities each has as husband and wife. Obvious? It is surprising how many letters I get groaning about these failures—each blaming the other. Self-righteousness is a menace to marriage.

4. *Communicate*. This is essential. One of the saddest things I have heard married people say is, "We don't really have anything to talk about anymore." I know of couples who remain silent with each other the entire day. In the restaurant, just look at a table next to you shared by a husband and wife. Often, nothing is said during the entire meal. A wonderful way to rekindle conversation is by discussing the Bible.

5. *Take time with each other.* For two people to get married only to go their separate ways is illogical and against God's plan for marriage. Modern life may appear to require perpetual running—I urge you to slow down.

6. *Give attention to the little things.* What do I mean by "little things"? It may be removing the curlers from your hair before your husband comes home. It may mean taking out the trash without protesting. *Simple things,* but oh so important.

7. *Beware of pitfalls and learn to forgive.* Each marriage is unique, and each faces its own peculiar problems. Recognize them and try to avoid them. But if they do occur— forgive. To have a successful marriage you need two good forgivers.

8. *Recognize the greatest enemy of your marriage—selfishness.* Have you ever asked yourself what the opposite of love is? Many of us would say, "hate." But this is an incomplete answer. The real opposite of love is selfishness. Being aware of this fact is an important step in the right direction. A happy marital partnership has to be dominated by love— two people seeking out ways to do what is best for the other.

9. *Learn to grow—together.* Too often one mate has matured remarkably but the other one is left far behind. Ruth and I have learned to listen carefully and respectfully to the other's point of view. We find it healing to kneel together at least once a day. I pray for her and she in turn prays for me. Let not the sun go down upon your wrath.

10. *See your marriage as an opportunity to serve.* God has not given us marriage just to be selfishly enjoyed. He wants us to use our marriage to benefit others. You will feel enriched when you do.

Billy stresses that each of the ten marriage commandments is only a starting point. "They can help prepare you for everlasting joy," he says. "That is, if you let them. Sadly, in our mixed-up system of values there is so much turmoil regarding the proper roles for husband and wife, father and mother. It's gotten so complicated that many couples do not know which way to turn. They regard the Bible as a stumbling block when it says, 'Wives, submit yourselves unto your husbands.'

"I try to tell them that 'submit' is only part of the passage. The full sentence is: 'Wives, submit yourselves unto your husbands, *as unto the Lord*.' I ask them to consider the word 'submit.' It means yield to authority and judgment of another. Its ancient root includes the implication that the partners are to adapt themselves to each other '*in the Lord*.'

"If the husband is 'in the Lord' his mind will be that of Jesus. Thus a husband is never first in the human family; that position rightfully belongs to God. The husband and wife have different functions but are equals in mind and conscience, position and privilege, freedom and happiness. Instead, many couples ignore that and battle about supremacy."

16
LIVING FOR EACH OTHER AND TOGETHER FOR GOD

"I LOVE RUTH far more now than I did when we were married," Billy confided. The evangelist and his wife believe without reservation that there is a simple explanation for their continuing ecstasy. To the Grahams, wedded bliss means *to live for each other and together for God*.

"A successful marriage is a triangle," Ruth says. "It consists of the husband, wife and the Lord. With that combination, marriage is made. It has been that way for me. Now that the children are grown and have families of their own, Bill and I are getting to spend more time together."

Recently, she joined her husband in London, where she watched Prince Philip award him the coveted $200,000 Templeton Prize in Religion. A usually reserved British journalist covering the posh event, which was held in Buckingham Palace, muttered, "Mrs. Graham should be emulated by all other wives. It's rather obvious that my wife didn't ogle me in that manner when I was named our borough's Outstanding Father of the Year."

That opinion is shared by many people who have observed the pair. Golda Meir, the late Premier of Israel, considered herself a good friend of the evangelist. "If he wasn't such a *goy*," she said jestingly when she was in her mid-seventies, "I'd try to catch him for a husband. But I'm afraid that Ruth would object, and I know what a hopeless job it would be to yank them apart. He gets stars in his eyes whenever he talks about her."

Billy has made many trips to the Holy Land, where he is held in high esteem by prominent Israeli officials. He disarmed them quickly by saying, "I'm very pro-Jewish. I feel close to the Jewish people. Christianity was built on Judaism. After all, we Christians have committed our lives to a Jew. . . . Whenever any group suffers injustice and oppression, the potential of a new holocaust exists. It would be blind optimism to declare it couldn't happen again."

Teddy Kollek, the fiery mayor of Jerusalem, said, "I know of no other Christian who is more dedicated an ally to us. I remember a trip I made with him to the Wailing Wall, the only surviving part of the Second Temple. We watched the *yarmulka*-wearing worshipers praying. Some of them were very, very old. There were tears in Billy's eyes."

Graham was extremely upset about the slaughter of Lebanese civilians by Christian Phalangist militiamen. He immediately told reporters that Israel should conduct a complete inquiry to determine how it was allowed to happen. He added that Americans should realize that the soldiers who committed the atrocity "are not Christians in our sense of the word." He emphasized that Christian Phalangist is a political term and not a religious name.

In between crusades the Grahams enjoy sitting on their porch and gently swaying in the handcarved rocking chairs President Johnson presented them. As they gaze across the valley 3600 feet below, to high mountain peaks, they frequently discuss world problems. Currently, the Middle East occupies a great deal of their concern. Ruth, who also feels close to the Jewish people, dangles a tiny lavaliere that she often wears. It's inscribed in Hebrew: "Pray for the peace at Jerusalem." She has stated repeatedly, "I simply can't understand how anyone who calls himself a Christian could be remotely anti-Semitic!"

Billy is not as worried about the United States or the Soviet Union dropping the atomic bomb as he is with the possible menace of a hostile and ambitious small country. "It's the tiny nation that is headed by an unstable leader that I fear the most."

He says that he gets some of his best thoughts during conversations with his wife: "I so look forward to spending quiet moments alone with her," he said recently. "Especially in our mountain home that seems so far removed from the hurry-scurry of the outside world. I've found that periods of tranquillity are so necessary for everyone's well-being. That's one of the things wrong with modern marriage—too much of 'you step on it, I'm in a hurry!' "

Billy has always liked to take long walks in the woods accompanied by one of his pet dogs. Belshazzar, a Great Pyrenees, was often at his side, and upon returning would boldly follow his master into the house. "That dog would never do that when Bill was away on a crusade," said Ruth. "But with Bill home, it was a completely different story. He idolized him—wouldn't leave his side. Why, he would get so jealous that once he ripped the coat of a visitor who had the effrontery to shake Bill's hand. Sometimes I wish there was such a thing as getting a dog converted."

A narrow, twisting, single-lane road winds up to the Graham's ten-room, cabin-style home. It was built of local hand-hewn logs and is encircled by an eight-foot electrified fence. Additional protection is provided by a sturdy iron-grille gate and three German shepherd police dogs. Ruth admits the security measures make her think of a concentration camp. "I always feel like apologizing to our guardian angels," she said.

J. Edgar Hoover recommended the high barrier and attack dogs when the evangelist and his family received kidnap threats. "In one week's time, five people tried to break into Billy's house," the F.B.I. director told a reporter from the *Washington Star*. "That's when I advised him that he better do something before tragedy struck. I proposed a sign saying: *Trespassers will be eaten*."

Johnny Cash is a close friend of the Grahams. "I'm afraid these safeguards are very necessary," he said. "My wife, June, and I also have been forced to install some precautions. Once you get past the ones Billy and Ruth have, you immediately think of heaven on earth. It's one of the most peaceful places June and I have ever visited. Simple, but at the same time inspiring. . . . Billy and Ruth are very serious about a German inscription that's burned into the mantel of their huge living room fireplace: *Ein feste Burg ist unser Gott*. It means, 'A mighty fortress is our God.' "

One intruder, a wild-eyed and disheveled man in his early twenties, managed to get into the house. He found Billy alone in the study. "I've come to kill you!" he shouted as he charged at the evangelist.

Graham wrestled him to the floor. Suddenly, the would-be assassin began to sob and babble unintelligible phrases. Billy realized that his unwelcome guest was mentally deranged. After calming him down and calling the authorities, he and the sick young man knelt down and prayed together.

An immense kitchen is the heart of the house. It, too, has a large fireplace. The walls and ceiling, like all the other rooms, have exposed timbers. The living room, dining room, book-lined study, and bedrooms are furnished with primitive mountain pieces now rated valuable antiques. "They are very rugged and have withstood the onslaught of energetic children and pets," Ruth said. "If we had bought delicate modern things, they would have worn out long ago. I was lucky to get them at a time when they were still available for insignificant sums. Today, we couldn't afford them."

She traveled the countryside, looking for mountain furniture, old beams and bricks. While saying, "Fill 'er up," she asked gasoline attendants if they knew of any abandoned cabins. The owner of a service station near Montreat recalled, "Mrs. Graham sure has a lot of native grit. She'd pounce on the slightest suggestion. One time I told her I thought a wooden bench was available down the road. I barely had time to get the nozzle out of her gas tank before she took off."

Several years ago Muhammad Ali visited the Grahams' mountain home. For more than five hours the former heavyweight boxing champion talked about what it was like to be a Muslim and discussed his fighting career. "I liked those two," Ali says. "But they are full of surprises. It started at the airport. I expected to be chauffeured in a Rolls-Royce or at least a Mercedes. But we got into this old American car and Billy drove it all by himself. The house also caught me by surprise. It's not a fancy mansion with crystal chandeliers and gold carpets. Just made out of plain old logs. Billy could probably make even more money than me, but I guess he likes what he's doing."

There has been widespread speculation about the value of the Graham estate. Estimates have ranged from $100,000 to several million. The evangelist shrugged his shoulders when replying. "The bank helped us raise money for the land. Book royalties and friends helped us build the house."

Early in Billy's career he decided to refuse the love offerings that traditionally provided income for traveling revivalists. By 1950 he had become a household name. For the past thirty years pollsters have rated him as one of the Ten Most Admired Men in the World. He was advised by Dr. Jesse Bader, Secretary of Evangelism for the National Council of Churches, to set up a nonprofit organization.

"What set me off," Graham recalls, "was two photographs in an Atlanta newspaper. One showed me waving good-bye to a crusade audience and the other showed a box of money the ushers had collected. They were featured side by side. The inference was pretty plain—I was conducting a racket. The image of Elmer Gantry was still large in many minds.

"I wanted no mistakes like that. So, to avoid any possible suspicion, I took Dr. Bader's advice and set up a corporation called the Billy Graham Evangelistic Association. I got a very competent board of directors, made the finances public and put myself on a straight salary. . . . I fear it's not enough to allow my family to sit back and enjoy a large inheritance."

The evangelist's initial salary was $15,000 a year. Currently he earns $39,500. He also receives royalties from his books. These funds are held in trust for Ruth and the children. The Grahams resolved they would never live higher than the pastor of a large city church. Close friends say that they have kept that vow. (The $200,000 Billy received when he was awarded the Templeton Prize was promptly donated to relief organizations and to schools which train evangelists.)

Shortly after Billy appeared on the cover of *Time* magazine, one of the children was asked, "Now, that your father is so famous, I suppose he'll buy you a large, talking doll."

The youngster shrugged her shoulders. "Who do you think he is," she replied, "Rockfeller?"

Whenever possible the Grahams visit their fifteen grandchildren. Several years ago Ruth was putting up a swing for her eldest daughter's youngsters. She leaned too far forward and fell out of a tall tree, which resulted in a concussion, memory loss and other severe injuries. Her right hip had to be reconstructed and surgery was performed on her wrist. For months she was forced to use a cane. She has abandoned motorcycle riding and hang-gliding, both sports she took up after reaching her fiftieth birthday.

Doctors restrict her to less vigorous activities. Among them are composing poetry, gardening, painting, sewing and traveling with her globe-trotting husband. Shortly after an earthquake struck Guatemala City, she and Billy flew there to coordinate relief work. Together they helped rebuild the devastated region. When they returned to the United States, the evangelist told a reporter, "I'm indeed fortunate to be married to a wife who has such deep-seated passion for people who aren't as lucky as we are. But then, many married men have wonderful helpmeets—they simply fail to recognize it. It doesn't have to be something as spectacular as an earthquake to make them realize their blessing."

Ruth has had a chronic cough for the past twenty years; it used to keep Billy awake. Not long ago she moved into a bedroom which adjoins his, but shyly admits that she's often in her husband's room. "Married couples need many moments together," she says.

Although the evangelist looks in splendid health, he has been hospitalized many times and suffers from a number of ailments. He has frequent disability from kidney stones, recurrent backache, high blood pressure and insomnia, and is subject to attacks of flu. Recently, he and his wife were scheduled to dine at the White House with President and Mrs. Reagan. The invitation had to be postponed when he slipped on a mountain ledge in Spokane, while hiking with his son Ned, and injured his lower back.

"A lesser man would have slowed down long ago," said one of his associates. "Doctors have warned him to take it easy. But not Billy Graham! He declared that God entrusted him with a mission and he's determined to carry it out no matter what. That man is a human spiritual dynamo—always on the move—always trying to operate full force. We have to constantly shield him or he'd attempt to work twenty-four hours a day. The president of the Southern Baptist Convention realized this when he said, 'I'm awfully glad the Lord is easier to get to than Billy is.'"

Dr. Martin Buehler, a distinguished Dallas physician, tried to impress upon the evangelist the pressing need to take better care of himself: "I insisted that he required more time off to rest and relax. I explained to him that no human body or mind could take the tremendous burden that he was constantly imposing on himself. I fear, however, that he listened with half an ear."

Billy did agree to make one concession: try and keep in shape by performing regular exercise. He run-walks every afternoon, and when he's at home during the warm weather, swims in a small pool that Ruth has built for him. "It's next to his bedroom," she explained, "and he doesn't have to walk far to use it. Not very big—four strokes by two strokes. He complained about the cost, but I told him that it's cheaper than a funeral."

Each September, Billy and Ruth take a two-week vacation. "It has become a ritual," says the evangelist. "We try to let nothing interfere with it. We go down to a little island in the Caribbean—St. John in the Virgin Islands. Believe me, by September we badly need the rest."

Several years ago their annual holiday afforded more than tranquillity and relaxation. Norman Lawrence, a fifty-one-year-old realtor from Maryland, tells why: "Marion, my wife, and I were vacationing at the Rockefeller place in St. John.

It was our twenty-fifth wedding anniversary, but it felt more like a hundred. To put it mildly, we weren't very contented with our lives.

"Not that we argued in public. No, we were too civilized for that. We were just plain bored! We'd sit through an entire meal without exchanging a word. It was the same when we were tennis partners or playing bridge. Even something simple like sneezing was ignored. It wouldn't occur to us to say, 'God bless you,' or to offer some other acknowledgment. Where the other one was concerned, we were strictly 'Silent Sam' and 'Silent Sue.'

"It was during one of our mute dinners that we saw the Grahams. Because they seemed so unlike us we kept staring at them. They were so animated. So alive. Then we did something we hadn't done in a long time—we actually talked to one another. We kept speculating why the Grahams liked being together. It was clear they had something we hadn't. It was Marion who suggested it was 'believing in the Lord.' I always wanted to be a good person—doesn't everybody? Perhaps this was the opportunity.

"Well, to make a long story short, we both became 'born-agains.' Marion doesn't like me using those words. She says that 'born-again' sounds like some kind of hellfire revivalism. She prefers 'conversion.' Feels that term is more accurate.

"Whatever you call it, we didn't honestly expect it to make much of a difference in our lives. But it has—honestly it has. It is still working—we're both happy to be in God's world. I don't want to sound saccharine, but I'm actually looking forward to our Golden Anniversary. And to think it all started by watching two people talk to each other!"

Billy is often asked, "Does being a public figure bother you?"

"Yes," replies the evangelist. "One of the most difficult things I have had to face was the loss of personal privacy. I did not seek the publicity, and how it all came about I truthfully don't know. I'd much rather be the minister of a small parish somewhere, but Ruth and I decided long ago that as it was this way, we'd go ahead with it. Years before I discovered that if your wife is behind what you're doing, the path becomes much smoother."

Billy evidenced his marital bliss in a television conversation with David Frost. "If a burglar was to get into your house somehow," asked the British talk show host, "and said he'd leave you one material possession or gift if you asked him nicely, what would you say you wanted to keep?"

Without hesitation, the evangelist replied, "My wife!"

Unmistakably, Ruth feels the same way. Some time ago a woman who was sitting next to her at a crusade gazed tenderly at the evangelist while he was speaking. "I wonder what it would be like to wake up and find yourself married to that man?" she said dreamily.

"You've asked the right person," Ruth replied. "I've been doing it for years. I tell you it's great and gets better all the time!"

BIBLIOGRAPHY

Allan, Thomas. *Crusade in Scotland*. London: Pickering and Inglis, 1955.

Babbage, Stuart, and Siggins, Ian. *Light Beneath the Cross*. Garden City, New York: Doubleday, 1960.

Barnhart, Joseph. *The Billy Graham Religion*. Philadelphia: United Church Press, 1972.

Bishop, Mary. *Billy Graham: The Man and His Ministry*. New York: Grosset and Dunlap, 1978.

Brown, Joan Windmill, editor. *Day by Day*. Minneapolis: World Wide Publications, 1976.

Burnham, George. *A Mission Accomplished*. Old Tappan, New Jersey: Fleming H. Revell, 1955.

―――. *To the Far Corners*. Old Tappan, New Jersey: Fleming H. Revell, 1956.

――― and Fisher, Lee. *Billy Graham and the New York Crusade*. Grand Rapids, Michigan: Zondervan Publishing House, 1957.

Colquhoun, Frank. *Haringey Story*. London: Hodder and Stoughton, 1955.

Cook, Charles. *The Billy Graham Story*. Wheaton, Illinois: Van Kampen Press, 1954.

———. *London Hears Billy Graham*. London: Marshall, Morgan and Scott, 1955.

Demary, Donald, editor. *Blow, Wind of God: Selected Writings of Billy Graham*. Grand Rapids, Michigan: Baker Book House, 1975.

Eisenhower, Julie Nixon. *Special People*. New York: Simon and Schuster, 1977.

Frady, Marshall. *A Parable of American Righteousness*. Boston: Little, Brown, 1979.

Frost, David. *Billy Graham Talks with David Frost*. Philadelphia: A. J. Holman, 1971.

Gillenson, Lewis. *Billy Graham and Seven Who Were Saved*. New York: Trident Press, 1967.

Graham, Billy. *The Secret of Happiness*. London World's Work, 1960.

———. *The Seven Deadly Sins*. Grand Rapids, Michigan: Zondervan Publishing House, 1955.

———. *Billy Graham Talks to Teenagers*. Grand Rapids, Michigan: Zondervan Publishing House, 1958.

———. *Billy Graham Answers Your Questions*. Minneapolis: World Wide Publications, 1960.

———. *The Challenge: Sermons from Madison Square Garden*. Garden City, New York: Doubleday, 1969.

———. *The Jesus Generation*. Grand Rapids, Michigan: Zondervan Publishing House, 1971.

———. *How to be Born Again*. Waco, Texas: Word Books, 1977.

Graham, Morrow. *They Call Me Mother Graham*. Old Tappan, New Jersey: Fleming H. Revell, 1977.

Graham, Ruth Bell, as told to Elizabeth Sherrill. *Our Christmas Story*. Minneapolis: World Wide Publications, 1971.

————. *Sitting by My Laughing Fire*. Waco, Texas: Word Books, 1977.

————. *It's My Turn*. London: Hodder and Stoughton, 1983.

High, Stanley. *Billy Graham*. New York: McGraw-Hill, 1956.

Hoke, Donald. *Revival in Our Time*. Grand Rapids, Michigan: Van Kampen Press, 1950.

Kilgore, James. *Billy Graham, the Preacher*. New York: Exposition Press, 1968.

Kooiman, Helen. *Transformed: Behind the Scenes with Billy Graham*. Wheaton, Illinois: Tyndale House, 1970.

McLoughlin, William. *Billy Graham: Revivalist in a Secular Age*. New York: Ronald Press, 1960.

McMahan, Thomas. *Safari for Souls: With Billy Graham in Africa*. Columbia, South Carolina: The State Record Company, 1960.

Mitchell, Curtis. *Billy Graham: The Making of a Crusader*. Philadelphia: Chilton Books, 1966.

————. *Billy Graham, Saint or Sinner*. Old Tappan, New Jersey: Fleming H. Revell, 1979.

Morris, James. *The Preachers*. New York: St. Martin's Press, 1973.

Parrot, L. Lee. *How to Be a Preacher's Wife and Like It*. Introduction by Ruth Graham. Grand Rapids, Michigan: Zondervan Publishing House, 1956.

Paul, Ronald. *Billy Graham: Prophet of Hope*. New York: Ballantine Books, 1978.

Poling, David. *Why Billy Graham?* Grand Rapids, Michigan: Zondervan Publishing House, 1977.

Pollock, John. *Billy Graham*. New York: McGraw-Hill, 1966.

————. *A Foreign Devil in China*. Minneapolis: World Wide Publications, 1971.

————. *Billy Graham, Evangelist to the World*. New York: Harper and Row, 1979.

Settel, T. S., editor. *The Faith of Billy Graham*. Anderson, South Carolina: Droke House, 1968.

Shea, George Beverly, with Bauer, Fred. *Then Sings My Soul*. Old Tappan, New Jersey: Fleming H. Revell, 1968.

Smart, W. J. *Six Mighty Men*. London: Hodder and Stoughton, 1956.

Strober, Gerald. *Graham: A Day in Billy's Life*. Garden City, New York: Doubleday, 1976.

——. *Billy Graham: His Life and Faith*. Waco, Texas: Word Books, 1977.

Tchividjian, Gigi Graham. *Thank You Lord, for My Home*. Minneapolis: World Wide Publications, 1980.

Wilson, Grady. *Billy Graham as a Teenager*.

Wirt, Sherwood Eliot. *Crusade at the Golden Gate*. New York: Harper and Row, 1959.

Index